Climate Change

Ulisse Di Corpo

www.sintropia.it

CONTENTS

WHAT THE PAST TELLS

We hear a lot about climate change. There is no doubt that temperatures, sea levels and CO_2 are increasing. But if we look at it from a broader perspective, the picture seems to be dramatically different. In this regard, the past can tell us a lot about what is happening today and about the future.

If we examine the data on carbon dioxide (CO_2) and temperatures that are available for the last 800 thousand years, we see that our planet goes through cycles of ice-age.

Before each ice-age the levels of CO_2 rise increasing the greenhouse effect.

All the countries that have research bases in the Antarctic have independently produced this data contained in ice cores.

Core drilling is a technique used for wells, for oil explorations or other excavation activities such as in archaeology for soil analyses. It consists in getting a cylindrical sample of the rock for analysis purposes and can be used also with the ice of the polar caps. Ice cores provide data on the weather conditions on Earth, from the current era backward to several hundred thousand years ago to almost a million years ago.

Ice cores show regular cycles of about one hundred thousand glacial years interspersed with just over ten thousand warm interglacial years. Every interglacial period is associated with increasingly higher levels of CO_2 and temperatures.

Ice maintains the same chemical properties that were present when snow fell and it is possible to distinguish the different years, in a way similar to the rings of the trunk of a tree. The air bubbles trapped in the these rings allow to establish and date the variations of methane, carbon dioxide, temperature and volcanic eruptions.

All the scientific bases in the Antarctica have produced similar results and no one is questioning them.

In the following graph it is possible to see the history of CO_2 and temperatures up to 400 thousand years ago.

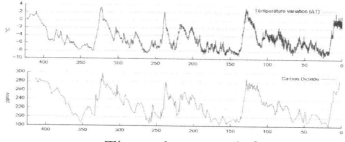

Thousands years ago [1] – [2]

We are at the right of the chart. The more we move to the left, the more we go back in time, until we reach four hundred thousand years ago. The numbers shown are relative to thousands of years ago.

Carbon dioxide (CO_2) is produced by life: breathing, the decomposition of plants and animals, the combustion of wood, coal, oil and gas. Without CO_2, trees and vegetation would not grow and life could not exist.

Together with water, CO_2 is the very essence of life! Life dies with ice and dies in the absence of CO_2!

CO_2 traps heat and this is essential to avoid

---

[1] en.wikipedia.org/wiki/Ice_age#/media/File:Vostok_Petit_data.svg
[2] cdiac.ornl.gov/images/air_bubbles_historical.jpg
cdiac.ornl.gov/trends/co2/ice_core_co2.html

low temperatures. Without the CO_2 invisible warm blanket that wraps around the planet life would be impossible. But, this "greenhouse effect" has never been enough to compensate for the lowering temperatures of the ice age.

CO_2 levels similar to or higher than the current ones indicate that in addition to natural sources, industrial civilized activities were also present.

Civilizations that preceded us in previous interglacial periods seem to have used CO_2 to counteract the reduction in temperatures of the ice age. But none were successful.

The scenario is quite simple! During the ice age temperatures fall by an average of 10/12 degrees. This drop in temperatures is slowed by high CO_2 levels. But when civilizations succumb to the ice age, CO_2 levels decrease and polar ice caps expand and reach thickness of 3 kilometers at latitudes like Rome and New York. Oceans levels decrease by 200/300 meters and civilizations are forced to migrate towards the equatorial strip and occupy the land that was previously covered by the oceans.

At the end of the ice age the increase in

temperatures is sudden. This causes the polar ice caps to melt into huge interglacial lakes. When the banks of these lakes break the levels of the oceans increase of tens of meters at a time, wiping out what was left of human civilizations. Reports of these floods can be found in all the traditions and date back to around 12,000 years ago.

The warm period in which we live began 12,000 years ago and now we are re-entering the next ice age.

In the last half century scientists have been warning that we are at the beginning of the next ice age. In 1972 the top US and European geologists concluded that the sediments of deep oceans show that the ice age has started and wrote to the president of the United States: *"The present rate of the cooling seems fast enough to bring glacial temperatures in about a century, if continuing at the present pace."*

Fortunately the ice age is still mitigated by the high levels of CO_2.

But, why are glacial cycles so regular?

Because the Sun is not constant in its emissions. Solar cycles were discovered in 1843 by Samuel Heinrich Schwabe who after 17 years of observations noted a periodic change in the average number of sunspots in a progression that follows an 11-year cycle.

Scientists were baffled by the fact that each cycle was a bit different and no model could explain these fluctuations.

In 2015 it was discovered that these fluctuations are caused by a double dynamo effect between two layers of the Sun, one near the surface and one inside its convection area. This model explains the irregularities of the past and predicts what will happen in the future.

Valentina Zharkova, one of the discoverers of this dynamo effect, describes the results in this way:

"We found magnetic waves that appear in pairs, originating from two different layers within the Sun. Both have a cycle of about 11 years, even if they are slightly out of phase. During the cycle, the waves float between the northern and southern hemispheres of the

Sun. Combining these waves and comparing them with the real data for the past solar cycles, we found that our predictions are 97% accurate."[3]

Using this model to predict the future we see that the pairs of waves will become increasingly out of phase during cycle 25, which reaches its peak in 2022. In cycle 26, which covers the decade from 2030 to 2040, the two waves will become totally out of phase and this will cause a significant reduction in solar emissions.

"In cycle 26, the two waves are opposed to each other, with their peak at the same time but in opposite hemispheres of the Sun. Their interference will be destructive and will cancel each other out ... when the waves are in phase, they can show a strong resonance, and we have strong solar activity. When they are out of phase, we have solar minima."

The last drop of 1.3 degrees Celsius in global temperatures led to the mini-glaciation of

---

[3] Royal Astronomical Society – *Irregular heartbeat of the Sun driven by double dynamo* https://www.ras.org.uk/news-and-press/2680-irregular-heartbeat-of-the-sun-driven-by-double-dynamo

1645-1715, a period known as the Maunder minimum, in which the hot seasons were short and there was a lack of food.

Zharkova expects a 60% drop in solar activity in the 2030-2040 period. The Sun is falling asleep and this is evident in the data available on www.spaceweatherlive.com

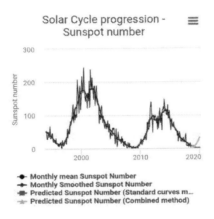

When solar emissions decrease, the magnetic shield that protects the Earth weakens and cosmic rays enter the core, activating magma, increasing earthquakes, volcanic eruptions and rains. More than a million volcanoes lie under the sea level against 15,000 on land. Eruptions of submarine volcanoes increase ocean temperatures, causing extreme weather conditions such as violent hurricanes and the rise in the amount of water vapor in the atmosphere.

The high levels of CO_2 of the previous interglacial periods suggests the existence of ancient intelligent and industrialized pre-glacial civilizations.

Are there traces of these civilizations?

Many archaeological discoveries cannot be explained and remain an enigma for experts. These findings are called *out of place artifacts* (OOPARTS). Artifacts that defy conventional chronology being too advanced for the level of civilization existing at the time, or because they show an intelligent presence before human beings.

In the book *"The Ancient Giants Who Ruled America: The Missing Skeletons and the Great Smithsonian Cover-Up"*[4] Richard Dewhurst

---

[4] Dewhurst R.J., *The Ancient giants Who Ruled America: The Missing Skeletons and the Great –Smithsonian Cover-Up*
https://www.amazon.com/gp/product/1591431719

presents evidence of an ancient race of giants in North America and the concealment by the Smithsonian Institution.

Thousands of skeletons of giants were found, particularly in the Mississippi Valley and also ruins of their cities. The book includes more than 100 photographs and illustrations and shows that the Smithsonian Institution came, took the skeletons for further study, and then made them disappear.

In some cases, other government institutions were involved. But the result was always the same: skeletons were removed and disappeared forever.

Why?

OOPARTS and pre-glacial civilizations contradict the narrative that we are the first civilization on this planet.

POSSIBLE SCENARIOS

In 1972 the chairman of the conference *The Present Interglacial, How and When Will it End*[5] which was held on 26 and 27 January 1972 at the Brown University, a leading research university, sent the following letter to President Nixon[6]:

December 3, 1972

Dear Mr President:

Aware of your deep concern with the future of the world, we feel obliged to inform you on the results of the scientific conference held here recently. The conference dealt with the past and future changes of climate and was attended by 42 top American and European investigators. We enclose the summary report published in Science and further publications are forthcoming in Quaternary Research.

The main conclusion of the meeting was that a global deterioration of climate, by order of magnitude larger than any

---

[5] Summary report of the conference *When Will the Present Interglacial End?* Science, 13 Oct 1972, Vol. 178, Issue 4057, pp. 190-202

[6] A copy of the letter is available at: realclimatescience.com/2017/11/the-history-of-the-modern-climate-change-scam/

hitherto experienced by civilized mankind, is a very real possibility and indeed may be due very soon. The cooling has natural cause and falls within the rank of processes which produced the last ice age. This is a surprising result based largely on recent studies of deep sea sediments.

Existing data still do not allow forecast of the precise timing of the predicted development, nor the assessment of the man's interference with the natural trends. It could not be excluded however that the cooling now under way in the Northern Hemisphere is the start of the expected shift. The present rate of the cooling seems fast enough to bring glacial temperatures in about a century, if continuing at the present pace.

The practical consequences which might be brought by such developments to existing social institutions are among others:

1) *Substantially lowered food production due to the shorter growing seasons and changed rain distribution in the main grain producing belts of the world, with Eastern Europe and Central Asia to be first affected.*
2) *Increased frequency and amplitude of extreme weather anomalies such as those bringing floods, snowstorms, killing frost etc.*

With the efficient help of the world leaders, the research could be effectively organized and could possibly find the answers to the menace. We hope that your Administration will take decisive steps in this direction as it did with other serious international problems in the past. Meantime however it seems reasonable to prepare the agriculture and industry for possible alternatives and to form reserves.

It might also be useful for Administration to take into
account that the Soviet Union, with larger teams monitoring the
climate change in Artic and Siberia, may already be considering
these aspects in its international moves.

With best regards,

George J. Kula
Lamont Doherty Geological
Observatory

R.K. Matthews, Chairman
Department of Geological
Sciences

Ice-core data and the double dynamo effect described by Valentina Zharkova show that we have already re-entered the next ice-age.

Valentina Zharkova points to 2032 when a strong drop of temperatures will provide an unequivocal sign that we are in the ice age.

However, it will take some-time before we fully get back into glacial temperatures and this will give time to get organized.

There are 3 possible scenarios:

1) Humanity will migrate towards the equatorial strip and built towns in the areas which were before covered by the oceans, since these areas are the warmest. But at the end of the ice age the ice caps will melt quickly and give place to interglacial lakes which will suddenly flood the ocean basins wiping away these remains of human civilizations. At the end only a small portion of humanity might survive and little traces of the previous civilizations and cultures will be left.

2) A small elite is concentrating huge resources and building advanced shelters which should allow a limited humanity to survive during the one hundred thousand years of glacial temperatures. This scenario is highly entropic and is inevitably doomed to failure.

3) Humanity as a whole will be able to face the ice-age and survive, but this requires the shift from the present highly entropic

and energy dissipative culture to a new culture that is syntropic and energy and heat concentrating.

This book is dedicated to the third scenario. A scenario which provides an incredible opportunity for the advancement of humanity.

The first scenario will not be described in this book. We will directly start from the second one and then focus on the third scenario.

SCENARIO #2: A SMALL ELITE

The scenario number 2 is that of a small elite which is planning to survive the ice age thanks to an incredible concentration of wealth and resources. As we will see this plan is doomed to failure and it is deeply damaging humanity as a whole.

This chapter describes how the concentration of wealth and resources is taking place. It might seem far away from the topic of climate change, but the intention is to save a small elite from the incoming ice age. It is useful to understand its rational in order to appreciate the third scenario, according to which humanity as a whole can survive the ice-age.

This mechanism of wealth and resources concentration is based on the fact that:
1. life continually exchanges matter, energy and information;
2. exchanges are vital for life;
3. exchanges require a medium.

In ancient Rome this medium was named *Linfa,* the divinity of fresh water that made nutrients available. In botany it is a liquid, which consists almost all of water, that flows from the roots upwards, through the conducting vessels that branch out into each leaf to reach the individual cells. In zoology the lymph is the liquid that circulates in invertebrates, also called hemolymph. In humans, the lymph is colorless or slightly yellowish and circulates in the lymphatic vascular system. Besides being mainly made of water, it contains proteins, lipids and lymphocytes.

The property of every lymph is to allow exchanges. Everything that allows exchanges becomes vital.

In human societies this function is provided by money. For this reason, money has a central position in the life of each person and each nation. Money is the lifeblood of society and anyone who controls money also controls the vital energy of people and nations.

But how does money work?

With the formation of States, coins were created as tools for the exchange of goods and services, as well as for the payment of taxes. The first coins were usually metal and were minted in large quantities. In modern economies coins have been accompanied by banknotes, which are easier and cheaper to produce and use.

Banknotes were introduced for the first time in 806 AD in China. People who had precious metals deposited them with the banks, for their preservation and protection from thieves, and the banks gave a receipt, a bank-note. Banknotes could be given to other people to collect the precious metals, even at another bank.

In Europe, the first account about banknotes was made by Marco Polo and the first banknotes appeared in 1661 in Sweden.

Banknotes were issued by commercial banks and were guaranteed by gold or silver coins.

In 1694, in England, commercial banknotes were replaced by national banknotes. This system devised by Charles Montagu gave birth to the first central bank: the Bank of England.

The Bank of England is the model on which Western central banks have been based.

In 1694, England could no longer finance the Nine-year war against France and Montagu planned that the debt-holding banks be brought together on the board of directors of the Bank of England, a private institution with long-term banking privileges, including the issue of banknotes. The Bank of England grouped the main commercial banks, in which the government had deposited valuables in exchange for banknotes.

The Bank of England gave banknotes in exchange for gold and applied an interest to cover the costs of the deposit and the security of the valuables.

Banknotes were therefore perceived as gold substitutes, since the conversion to gold was certain.

This initial phase was called the gold standard. The gold standard allowed anyone to go to the central bank and convert the banknotes into gold. At the same time, gold could be imported and exported freely.

The British government, thanks to its military power and its empire, was able to impose the gold standard as the ideal model of the international monetary system. Its advantages were undeniable. First of all, its intrinsic ability to stabilize the exchange rates between the various currencies of the countries participating in this system. If a country had a trade deficit, the currency depreciated and the balance recovered. If there was a trade surplus, the currency appreciated and the surplus diminished. The gold standard was therefore a very effective system.

However, private central banks concentrated immense power and wealth in the hands of a few greedy and unscrupulous bankers.

The war for independence of the United States of America was mainly a war of independence from the Bank of England.

To prevent America from falling again under the dictatorship of a few greedy bankers, the founding fathers of the United States prohibited in the first article of the constitution the establishment of a private central bank.

In the United States the first institution with central bank responsibilities was started in 1791 by Alexander Hamilton. But article 1, section 8 of the United States Constitution prohibits the formation of private central banks:

"Only the Congress shall have power ... to coin money, regulate the value thereof."

Consequently, in 1836 President Andrew Jackson (1829-1837) declared the Bank of the United States an unconstitutional aberration and an affront to popular sovereignty, as it concentrated extraordinary powers in the hands of a small group of bankers not elected by the people, and abolished the Bank of the United States, claiming that it exercised a negative influence on the economy and the country.

Without a central bank each commercial bank could print its banknotes, secured by Treasury bonds.

But this made the dollar unattractive compared to the British pound that was used in international transactions.

A war started between bankers. The Astor, Guggenheim and Straus, the most powerful bankers of the time, were strong supporters of the first article of the constitution and were against the establishment of a central bank. Instead, the Rockefellers, Morgan and Rothschild pushed for the establishment of a private central bank.

In 1912 President William Taft continued to veto the establishment of a central bank. But, oddly enough, the bankers who opposed the establishment of a central bank (the Astor,

Guggenheim and Straus) all died on April 15, 1912 in the sinking of the Titanic, the largest ocean liner in service at the time. The bankers who favored the creation of the central bank were late and did not get on board.

Soon after, on December 23, 1913, the newly elected president Woodrow Wilson signed the Federal Reserve Act. A congressional act that established the Federal Reserve System (FED), the central banking system of the United States, which centralized the US financial system in a privately owned entity.

Only the FED was authorized to print dollars, regulate interest rates, money supply, credit creation and inflation. The FED could lend money to the government and ask for an interest.

To overcome the fierce debate on central banks and the prohibition of article 1, section 8 of the US Constitution, the word *"Federal"* was intentionally used to give the impression that the FED is a public entity.

This false impression is still used on the FED website.

"The Federal Reserve System fulfills its public mission as an independent entity within government. It is not owned by anyone and is not a private, profit-making institution."[7]

In 1914, when the FED started printing the first banknotes, the international trading system was under the rule of the British pound. But, only eight months later, in August 1914, the First World War transformed the dollar into the main international currency. The United States remained neutral until April 1917, when it declared war on Germany.

With the war, the US government spending increased fifteen times, causing it to borrow from the FED. The same happened to the European allies and the FED favored the indebtment of nations by lending the dollars generously.

Public spending had exceeded tax revenues in all countries.

US war bonds were issued to raise additional funds and the FED assumed a central role

---

[7] https://www.federalreserve.gov/faqs/about_14986.htm

facilitating their sale.

By the spring of 1918, about $10 billion of war bonds were placed. The large recourse to loans and the ample supply of money caused the public debt to surge.

At the end of World War I, the FED had become the main player on the world stage and the dollar was the main currency guaranteed by the gold that Europe had sent in the FED's coffers to repay ammunition, weapons and US exports.

When the war hit Europe in 1914, the huge military expenditures forced the European nations to abandon the gold standard. The excess of banknotes that was printed could no longer be guaranteed by gold. This made the British pound and other European currencies unstable and traders were forced to use the dollar as a medium of exchange.

The war made trade credits more difficult to obtain and dollars had to be used all over the world to finance commerce. This dramatically increased the power and centrality of the FED.

At the end of World War I, President Woodrow Wilson, who had signed the Federal

Reserve Act, declared:

"I am a most unhappy man. I have unwittingly ruined my country. A great industrial nation is controlled by its system of credit. Our system of credit is concentrated. The growth of the nation, therefore, and all our activities are in the hands of a few men. We have come to be one of the worst ruled, one of the most completely controlled and dominated governments in the civilized world. No longer a government by free opinion, no longer a government by conviction and the vote of the majority, but a government by the opinion and duress of a small group of dominant men."[8]

The debt ensured the control of European nations by the FED. After the United States entered World War I, the allies (mainly England and France) received loans amounting to $8.8 billion. The total sum of war debts, including loans granted in the period 1919-1921, was over $11 billion.

The German industrialists began to sabotage

---

[8] Woodrow W. *"The New Freedom"*, Doubleday Page Company, 1918, New York, under the chapter IX titled: BENEVOLENCE, OR JUSTICE?

all the obligations to repay war debts. They refused to pay taxes and moved capitals abroad. This led to a deficit in the state budget that was covered by the issuance of unsecured marks causing hyperinflation. In November 1922 the American dollar was worth 320 marks, a year later in November 1923 it was worth 4,210,500,000,000 marks. The collapse of the German currency caused considerable political instability, the occupation of the Ruhr by foreign troops and the misery of the population.

In 1924 the American banker Charles G. Dawes was commissioned by the Committee for Allied Repairs to investigate the problem. His report, published in April 1924, proposed a plan to establish annual debt repair payments on a fixed scale. He also recommended the reorganization of the German State Bank into a private central bank. In the summer of 1924, the "Dawes plan" was adopted at the London conference.

In August 1924, the old German mark was replaced by a new stabilized banknote.

The gold that Germany had paid in the form

of war reparations was acquired by the FED and returned to Germany in the form of an "aid" plan, granted by England and France, in turn to pay the war debt. This aid plan was covered with interests. In the end, all the German population lived in debt, under the blackmail of the FED that could withdraw its loans at any time and cause complete bankruptcy.

An unstoppable tide of FED banknotes poured into Germany in the form of foreign investments which in the period 1924-1929 amounted to almost 63 billion gold marks. In 1929 the German industries were in second place in the world. But they were largely in the hands of major American financial groups. American cooperation with the German military-industrial complex was so intense that in 1933 the key sectors of German industries and large banks such as Deutsche Bank, Dresdner Bank and Donat Bank were under the control of the FED.

In 1922 a meeting between Adolf Hitler and the US military attaché in Germany, Captain Truman, took place in Munich. Immediately afterwards, a financial miracle occurred for the Nazi party. Following substantial donations from abroad, in September 1930 the Nazi party obtained 6.4 million votes, thus winning the second place in the Reichstag.

Heinrich Brüning, former German chancellor, wrote in his memoirs:

"... since 1923, Hitler received large sums from abroad. Where they went is unknown, but they were received through Swiss and Swedish banks."

Louis McFadden, Republican Member of the United States House of Representatives from 1915 to 1935, principal sponsor of the McFadden Act of 1927, described the FED with the following words:

"Some people think that the Federal Reserve Banks are United States Government institutions. They are private monopolies which prey upon the people of the United States for the benefit of themselves and their foreign customers; foreign and domestic speculators and swindlers; and rich and predatory money lenders."

In the book *"A Monetary History of the United States"*, Milton Friedman and Anna Schwartz[9] show that in the autumn of 1929 the FED intentionally reduced the money supply triggering the collapse of the US stock market and provoking the Great Depression.

The power of the FED had become a danger to the United States and several bankers, along with the US Treasury, were starting an alternative monetary system based on banknotes secured by the silver of the US Treasury (*silver certificates*).

Friedman and Schwartz wrote:

"From the cyclical peak in August 1929 to a cyclical trough in March 1933, the stock of money fell by over a third."

The result was what Friedman calls the *"Great Contraction"*, a period of falling prices and employment caused by the limited monetary supply.

The American economy had already gone

---

[9] Friedman M. and Schwartz A.J., "A Monetary History of the United States, 1867-1960", ISBN: 9781400829330

through a series of expansion and contraction cycles.

Depressions often seemed to be triggered by banking panic, the most significant occurred in 1873, 1893, 1901 and 1907. Before the establishment of the FED, the banks had faced these crises by suspending the convertibility of currency deposits and since 1893 the financial institutions intervened during these crises by providing liquidity to the banks, thus reducing the panic that would have led to the depression and bankruptcy of the banks.

But in 1928-32 the FED did not provide liquidity to the banks. Indeed, the policy of monetary contraction contributed to the bank crisis, causing the bankruptcy of one-third of all US banks and their forced liquidation at very low prices with the selling of their assets. To be more precise, all the banks that were working on the new silver dollar monetary system were swept away by the great depression. Silver certificate dollars disappeared and the FED again had the monopoly of the currency.

The banking crisis and economic depression in the United States spread to central Europe and, in September 1931, England abandoned the gold standard thus destroying the international payment system and completely cutting off the financial oxygen for the Weimar Republic.

On January 4, 1932, a meeting was held between the major English financiers, Adolf Hitler and von Papen. This meeting was also attended by US politicians and the Dulles brothers, something their biographers do not like to mention.

On January 14, 1933, a meeting took place between Hitler, Schröder, Papen and Keplero, where Hitler's program was fully approved. It was at this meeting that the question of transferring powers to the Nazis was finally resolved, and on January 30th Hitler became Chancellor.

The attitude of the Anglo-American government circles towards the new German government was very understanding. When Hitler refused to pay war debts, neither Britain nor France made any claims. Furthermore, the Reichsbank, the German central bank, was now a private and independent central bank. In

May 1933 it was given a loan of $1 billion and the cessation of payments of old debts and in June England assigned $2 billion.

Thus, the Nazis got what the Weimar Republic failed to achieve.

In the summer of 1934, Britain signed the Anglo-German agreement which became one of the bases of British politics towards the Third Reich, and in the late 30s Germany became England's main trading partner. As Hitler himself admitted, his four-year plan was possible thanks to the loans he received from abroad.

In August 1934, the American Standard Oil bought 730,000 acres of land in Germany and built large oil refineries that supplied the Nazi regime. At the same time, the Nazis received the most modern technologies from the United States, including military patents by the American companies Pratt & Whitney, Douglas and Curtis Wright which were used to build the Junkers-87, the military bombers that the Luftwaffe used during the Second World War.

In 1941, when the Second World War raged,

US investments in the German economy amounted to $475 million. Standard Oil invested $120 million, General Motors $35 million, ITT $30 million and Ford $17.5 million.

The close economic and financial cooperation of the Anglo-Americans and the Nazis was the basis of the policy that led to the Second World War.

When the United States entered the war, the FED declared that it was:

"…prepared to use its powers to assure at all times an ample supply of funds for financing the war effort."

Financing the war was at the core of the FED's policies.

Before the war, the US military was small and its weapons were obsolete. The military needed to buy thousands of ships, tens of thousands of airplanes, hundreds of thousands of vehicles, millions of cannons and hundreds of millions of bullets and ammunition. The military needed to recruit, train and deploy millions of soldiers on six continents.

These tasks involved the payment of entrepreneurs, inventors and companies so that they, in turn, could buy supplies, pay workers and produce weapons with which American soldiers would defeat their enemies.

Military spending increased from a few hundred million dollars a year before the war to $85 billion in 1943 and $91 billion in 1944 (equivalent to $1.3 trillion in 2018).

The plans to finance the war were devised by the FED and were based on the marketing of bonds that fit the possibilities of all budgets, from small savers to large companies.

The FED organized the Victory Fund committees and developed collaborations with banks, companies and volunteers.

To support the financing of the war, the FED asked the Congress to amend the Federal Reserve Act by allowing it to buy government bonds in unlimited amounts, without guaranteed deposits, thus indebting the US government beyond any measure.

At the end of World War II the gold standard no longer existed, and between 1 and 22 July 1944, 730 delegates from the 44 countries that were winning the war gathered at the Mount Washington Hotel in Bretton Woods, New Hampshire, in the United States, to redefine a new international monetary order.

The famous British economist John Maynard Keynes proposed the creation of an international currency issued by an international central bank, a world body with the power to print banknotes. However, the idea was strongly opposed by the US delegation, and in particular by its leading economist Harry Dexter White, who referred to his country's military superiority.

Keynes's proposal, supported by the United Kingdom, to introduce a supranational currency did not prevail over the interests of the FED.

The outcome of the Bretton Woods conference was to give the US dollar the role of the only international currency.

It took three weeks, but eventually the Bretton Woods delegates had to accept the full triumph of the FED. The gold standard was limited to the dollar which had a fixed value against gold of $35 per ounce. All other currencies were tied to the dollar with a fluctuation between the currencies of 10%. The only limitation was due to the fact that each country could ask the FED to exchange dollars for gold kept at Fort Knox.

The dollar acquired a role of growing international hegemony and was used in all important transactions, from food to raw materials, metals and, of course, for the purchase and sale of oil, which at that time proved to be the most strategic market.

The dollar was the only currency guaranteed by gold and the only currency that could be used in international transactions! The only reserve currency!

The American president John Fitzgerald Kennedy was well aware of this situation of excessive power of the FED and with his executive order 11110 of 4 June 1963, he tried to rebalance the monetary policy by authorizing the Treasury of the United States of America to issue banknotes guaranteed with silver deposits.

The intention was to move the monetary control from the FED to the Treasury.

JOHN F. KENNEDY
XXXV *President of the United States: 1961-1963*

Executive Order 11110—Amendment of Executive Order No. 10289 as Amended, Relating to the Performance of Certain Functions Affecting the Department of the Treasury
June 4, 1963

By virtue of the authority vested in me by section 301 of title 3 of the United States Code, it is ordered as follows:

SECTION 1. Executive Order No. 10289 of September 19, 1951, as amended, is hereby further amended —

(a) By adding at the end of paragraph 1 thereof the following subparagraph (j):

"(j) The authority vested in the President by paragraph (b) of section 43 of the Act of May 12, 1933, as amended (31 U.S.C. 821 (b)), to issue silver certificates against any silver bullion, silver, or standard silver dollars in the Treasury not then held for redemption of any outstanding silver certificates, to prescribe the denominations of such silver certificates, and to coin standard silver dollars and subsidiary silver currency for their redemption," and

(b) By revoking subparagraphs (b) and (c) of paragraph 2 thereof.

SEC. 2. The amendment made by this Order shall not affect any act done, or any right accruing or accrued or any suit or proceeding had or commenced in any civil or criminal cause prior to the date of this Order but all such liabilities shall continue and may be enforced as if said amendments had not been made.

JOHN F. KENNEDY
THE WHITE HOUSE,
June 4, 1963

"Silver dollars" were issued without interest and did not indebt the government.

They were similar to the FED banknotes, with the difference that they were labeled "Silver Certificate" while the FED banknotes were marked "Federal Reserve Note" and the seal and the serial number instead of being green were red.

Five months later, on November 22, 1963, Kennedy was assassinated and the 4 billion *"Silver Certificate"* Treasury notes were immediately withdrawn, giving the FED full control of the dollar again.

At this point the FED had also total control of the government, the media and the US military establishment.

Communist countries had not submitted to the FED's dictatorship and had become number one enemies. This justified the Vietnam war which caused massive debt.

In 1959 the US foreign deficit and the gold reserve amounted to about 20 billion dollars, by 1967 the deficit had reached 36 billion and the gold reserves had fallen to 12 billion, due to the increasing requests for conversion of dollars in gold from some central banks.

On August 15, 1971, Richard Nixon made the unilateral decision to end the Bretton Woods agreements. The gold reserves of the United States had fallen to a fraction of the foreign debt, while requests for conversion of dollars into gold had become unstoppable. The gold standard was replaced by a flexible exchange system, while the institutions created at Bretton Woods survived. The International Monetary Fund and the World Bank are still in business and the GATT was replaced in 1995 by the WTO, the World Trade Organization.

At this point the world monetary system had to move from private central banks to state central banks, but the overwhelming US military superiority along with the interests of the oligarchs that controlled the FED led to the birth of the petrodollars.

The gold standard was transformed into the petrodollar standard where the dollar was guaranteed by oil. The United States began to impose this system based on private central banks, on the supremacy of the dollar and on its exclusive use in the purchase and sale of oil.

The first nation that was sanctioned for violating this policy was Chile. Salvador Allende, elected in November 1970, had nationalized the central bank. The reaction was swift. On 11 September 1973, the world witnessed one of the bloodiest coups.

In 1974 the petrodollar system was formalized in an agreement between the US administration and the Saudi regime which sanctioned the de facto equivalence between dollars and oil. Under this agreement, Saudi Arabia could only sell its oil in dollars and the surplus, about 70%, had to be used to buy US treasury bonds. This agreement signed with the Saudis was soon extended to all other oil-producing countries. The countries that imported oil were thus obliged to keep vast reserves of dollars.

The second oil crisis, that of 1979, was used to reinforce the hegemonic role of the dollar. Crude oil prices increased by 250% and the FED reacted with a significant rise in interest rates, attracting a huge flow of capitals.

The developing countries had already been drained by the debt created by international organizations. In Europe, public debt was limited by laws that prevented borrowing money from central banks. But in the mid-1970s central banks managed to circumvent these laws and began to buy all the treasury bonds that were not placed. In this way they could finance an unlimited public debt.

Within a few years, taxes were no longer used to finance public spending, but to pay interests on the debt. Citizens and nations were forced to sell their properties to pay interests on the debt and entire nations were subjugated.

In 2000, Saddam Hussein challenged this system, nationalizing the Iraqi central bank and selling oil in currencies other than the dollar. Economic sanctions and war were immediate. Other countries, including Syria, Libya, Venezuela, Russia, Iran and Indonesia, began to consider the nationalization of their central banks and the use of currencies other than the dollar for the sale of oil.

Anyone trying to break away from the petrodollar system and the FED dictatorship knew they would suffer the same fate as Saddam Hussein.

Mu'ammar Gaddafi tried to break away from this system by establishing a supranational currency, the gold dinar, which would have unified Africa under the same currency, pushing it away from private central banks and debts. Support was widespread, but the revolutions of the 2011 Arab Spring in North Africa and the assassination of Gaddafi stopped this project.

In 2005, Iranian President Ahmadinejad Mahomoud announced that the small island of Kirsh would soon host a stock exchange for hydrocarbons where oil and other hydrocarbons would be traded in euros or other currencies, but not dollars. Henry Kissinger summarized in an August 2006 interview: *"If Tehran insists a military confrontation with America is inevitable."*

On December 8, 2007, the central bank of Iran, which is a public institution, officially announced its decision to convert all oil payments into currencies other than the dollar.

On 17 February 2008, shortly after the

meeting in Davos, the Kirsh Stock Exchange was officially presented and became operational on 18 July 2011. On 31 December 2011, Obama signed a law requiring the United States Congress to punish any organization having financial transactions with the central bank of Iran, thus reaffirming the prohibition of breaking away from the system of petrodollars, the FED and private central banks.

In 2018 Vladimir Putin was re-elected president of the Russian Federation. One of the objectives of his mandate is to bring the Russian central bank under parliamentary control.

The monetary system of private central banks is based on a scam.

Imagine a central bank (ie a typographer) commissioned by a match organizer to print 10,000 tickets.

The printing of 10,000 tickets costs $50. But the central bank does not ask for the cost of printing, it asks for the value printed on the ticket (on the bill). If it prints 10,000 banknotes of $10 it asks for $100,000 in Treasury bonds, based on the fact that the banknotes "are worth" $10 each.

It is true that they are worth $10 each, but their value does not depend on the number printed on the banknote, but on their demand. The central bank knows this, but blackmail the organizers, the politicians, promising a generous gift to support their candidacy in the upcoming elections. On the contrary, it will fund other candidates and discredit those honest people who have opposed this system. This is what happens in all countries where central banks are private.

Those who own central banks usually control mass media and legislators and this gives them total power over the nations.

Henry Ford said:

"It is well enough that people of the nation do not understand our banking and monetary system, for if they did, I believe there would be a revolution before tomorrow morning."

- The debt scam

The *2008 Emergency Economic Stabilization Act*, commonly referred to as a bailout of the U.S. financial system, a law enacted in response to the subprime mortgage crisis, which authorized the United States Secretary of the Treasury to spend $700 billion to purchase distressed assets, especially mortgage-backed securities, and supply cash directly to banks, can be seen as the last step of a premeditated strategy aimed to drastically increase the public debt.

The Act was proposed by Treasury Secretary Henry Paulson during the global financial crisis of 2008, it was signed into law by President George W. Bush on October 3 and immediately ratified by the newly elected president, Barak Obama.

With this act the public debt was massively increased with money borrowed from the FED. In the period 2008-2011 the FED gave more than $17 trillion to US and European banks, by far more than the GDP (Gross

Domestic Product).

Few historians tell that the subprime mortgage crisis was skillfully prepared with the repeal of the *Glass–Steagall Act* in 1999.

The Glass-Steagall Act had proved fundamental in solving the Great Depression of 1929.

The Great Depression shook the world economy and lead to a sharp reduction of international trade, income, tax revenues, prices and profits. Major cities around the world were badly hit, the construction sector halted, the agricultural and rural areas suffered from the collapse of prices, mining and forestry areas saw a dramatic drop in demand for natural resources and raw materials.

The beginning of the Great Depression occurred on 24 October 1929 (Black Thursday) with the crisis of Wall Street, which was followed by the final collapse of securities on 29 October (Black Tuesday) that provoked a wave of panic among small investors, who rushed to withdraw their savings from banks.

The withdrawal of money from banks caused the failure of many banks which were forced to close or scale back. Industrial production fell by almost 50%, layoffs increased unemployment and consumption declined.

The economy was almost completely paralyzed.

The Glass-Steagall Act was passed by the Congress of the United States of America on 16 June 1933, in order to solve the problems that led to the Great Depression, limiting commercial bank securities activities and affiliations between commercial banks, investment banks and securities firms. It established the Federal Deposit Insurance Corporation (FDIC), an independent agency of the federal US government created to maintain stability and public confidence, which guarantees the deposit accounts of commercial banks and thus avoids the panic and rush to withdraw savings which had triggered the great Depression.

The distinction between investment banks, that gain on stocks and securities, and commercial banks, that produce revenues managing deposits, was based on the principle that hazards must be at your own risk. Bankers were forbidden to hold positions in investment banks and commercial banks.

Who worked in securities could not hold positions in commercial banks.

The government guaranteed deposits of commercial banks, but not the activities of investment banks.

The Glass-Steagall Act was repealed in 1999 with the Gramm-Leach-Bliley Act that cancelled the distinction between investment banks and commercial banks and removed the conflict of interest that prevented bankers of investment banks to work also for commercial banks.

The Gramm-Leach-Bliley Act, introduced in the Senate as the Financial Service Modernization Act removed the prohibitions of the Glass-Steagall Act and opened the way to the speculative use of savings and deposit accounts, forcing the Government to intervene in the rescue of investment banks (as it then happened in the 2008 bailout act).

The distinction between investment and commercial banks had been introduced in all

Western countries and was gradually removed starting from the beginning of the 1990s.

In Italy the distinction between commercial banks and investment banks had been established by the Banking Law of 1936 which defined the banking system of public interest. In 1993 this distinction was cancelled with the Banking Act, which introduced the concept of the Universal Bank, and repealed the distinction between commercial banks and investment banks by effectively shifting the risk of financial investments to the State.

The merge between commercial banks and investment banks allowed the flow of large amounts of money into stock exchanges. Stock prices soared, attracting the savings of millions of families. However, in early March 2000 the rise of the dot-com stocks suddenly stopped and shortly after share prices started to fall ever more rapidly.

At the same time real estate prices, which had stagnated for nearly a decade, began to rise, while mortgages were offered at very low rates to people without guarantees (the subprime mortgages that almost anyone could receive).

American families, deprived of their savings by the fall of dot-com stock prices, moved towards real estate investments in the belief that, unlike dot-com, these would be safe investments.

Interest rates remained low until 2005. This led to a gradual and steady growth in property values, together with a gradual and steady growth of subprime mortgages and of the debt of American house owners.

In 2006, with the succession of Ben Bernanke to Alan Greenspan at the head of the FED, interest rates began to rise, and mortgages suddenly became expensive causing the first signs of difficulties for indebted families. Real estate markets began to stagnate and families suddenly found themselves with mortgages that were worth more than the property they had purchased. Families who were no longer able to pay the ever-increasing mortgages rates declared bankruptcy.

Banks were forced to tighten loans terms, making it harder for people to get and renew mortgages, in the belief that house prices would keep falling and the economy would continue to slow.

The credit crunch depressed the real estate market and reduced the liquidity of house owners, raising unemployment and triggering insolvency.

The repeal of the Glass-Steagall Act allowed the securitization, the transformation of subprime mortgages into bonds, thus leading people and banks to buy bonds which were not redeemable, the famous toxic assets. These securities were sold around the world, often mixed with low-risk investments. The growing insolvency of house owners froze these bonds and plagued the banking systems.

The subprime crisis broke out in the U.S. in August of 2007, but securitization caused the crisis to occur officially on 16 September 2008 with the bankruptcy of Lehman Brothers. The failure of Lehman Brothers marked the beginning of the collapse of the financial markets and of soaring interbank rates. Millions of Americans lost their jobs. The prospect of a generalized crisis and of the meltdown of the financial systems forced the American presidents (Bush and immediately after Obama) to intervene with a rescue program (Bank Bailout), which increased in one day the indebtment by $700 billion.

In this way the bank debt was nationalized and spread over all U.S. citizens. Europe followed suit, suddenly increasing the public debt.

The repeal of the Glass-Steagall Act has given rise to derivatives which have reached the stratospheric figure of more than $700 trillion, compared to a world GDP of $63 trillion (as at June 2011).

The subprime mortgage crisis which started in the United States in August 2007, brought major banks to the brink of bankruptcy.

During the annual World Economic Forum in Davos, 2008, internationally renowned bankers demanded that their banks be nationalized.

The United States and other governments, first of all Britain, instead of nationalizing the banks, nationalized their debts.

Debts became public, but gains remained private. Almost all banks were saved unconditionally.

When the topic is the welfare of the citizens, governments consistently refuse to spend public money, whereas for the debts of the banks there are no limits in allocating public money and spreading the debt on the community.

On 5 December 2008, the FED had provided the U.S. banking system $1.2 trillion, with the Financial Stability Board, whose rules were dictated not by governments but by the bankers and brokers who caused the crisis. Bankers imposed their rules.

A huge amount of money was converted into public debt. In 2008 the bank bailout, the nationalization of the debt of the banks, led nations already stifled by a strong debt to find themselves faced with the specter of default, a situation unimaginable just a few years before.

Policies of *"tears and blood"* included tax increases, reduced welfare, later retirement age and reduction in the protection of workers.

On 21 February 2012, Greece reached an agreement with the Troika, the European Central Bank (ECB), the International Monetary Fund (IMF) and the European

Union (EU), in order to receive €130 billion.

Greece was forced to add another €107 billion reduction of interest on loans previously granted, which meant a loss of more than 70% in the savings of individuals who had Greek bonds

According to the Troika, these policies were intended to reinvigorate the Greek economy, but they took the economy to the brink of default, allowing in the meantime banks and financial institutions to regain their money and a good slice of the Hellenic sovereignty.

In exchange for financial aid the Troika requested the inclusion of a provision in the Greek Constitution which gives repaying the debt absolute priority over any other type of public spending (health, schools, pensions), and which will allow banks and financial institutions to seize the immense Greek heritage (cultural and natural), reducing the people into a state of semi-slavery and extreme poverty, with the creation of low cost labor.

This situation decreased the Hellenic GDP and increased public debt, making it even more dramatic.

Only ten days after the agreement between Greece and the Troika, Moody's cut Greece's rating to "junk", reducing it from Ca to C, the last step before default. Similarly Standard & Poor's cut Greece's rating to "selective default", whereas Fitch reduced it from C to CCC stating in this way "default in the short term."

Before the banking crisis, Greek public debt was equal to 112% of GDP, it is now over 180% and it is expected to rise as a result of the measures imposed by the ECB and IMF.

These measures are strongly recessive and lead to decrease the denominator (GDP) and, consequently, the proportion of public debt becomes greater, making the Greek crisis even more serious and unmanageable.

In *Postcapitalism a Guide Tour to Our Future* Paul Mason states:

"After the left party Syriza won the election in January 2015, the European Central Bank, whose job was to promote the stability of the Greek banks, pulled the plug on those banks, triggering €20 billion run on

deposits. That forced the left-wing government to choose between bankruptcy and submission. You will find no minutes, no voting record, no explanation for what the ECB did. It was left to the right-wing German newspaper Stern to explain: they had smashed Greece... Then I watched euphoria turn to anguish as a population that had voted left for the first time in seventy years saw its democratic wishes trashed by the European Central Bank... the struggle for justice collided with the real power that runs the world... The Central Banks, whose operations most people have no clue about, are prepared to sabotage democracy by triggering bank runs where anti-neoliberal movements threaten to win – as they did with Cyprus in 2013, then Scotland and now Greece... the bad news is that they control nearly every government in the world."

In this system illnesses, wars, conflicts, tensions and natural disasters provide value to money, and this is the reason behind the limitless amount of money that is allocated for wars and for crises that predate on people and nations, whereas there is always no or little money for the promotion of wellbeing.

With the advent of Internet, Iceland became a paradise for investment banks that offered high interest rates. This formula attracted a considerable amount of foreign capital, which in 2007 exceeded by nine times the Icelandic gross domestic product.

With the 2008 meltdown of the financial markets, investment banks entered in a crisis, and the conservative Prime Minister Geir Haarde did not hesitate to nationalize their debt, thus transforming a private debt, nine times greater than the GDP of the country, into a public debt.

The Icelandic króna was immediately devalued by 85%, thereby increasing the foreign debt of the online investment banks to more than 90 times the Icelandic GDP.

To repay this debt Iceland obtained a loan of over $2 billion from the International Monetary Fund and other $2 billion from countries of northern Europe. In return it had to enforce austerity measures and to impose a tax of more than 18,000 euro for each Icelandic citizen, including children. This tax would have been paid in 15 years at an interest rate of 5.5% per year.

The international financial authorities urged to adopt more drastic measures which would have reduced civil rights and the welfare of Icelanders. At this point citizens started a popular uprising.

The Icelanders did not understand why they should pay the debt contracted by financial speculators who became rich beyond belief with their unscrupulous investments. Why should the debt contracted by these unscrupulous bankers and brokers fall on the citizens? Why did the Icelandic government not ask the bankers to return the money they had stolen from the investment banks?

The Icelanders rejected the idea that the debt of these private banks could be transferred and become a sovereign debt which would have sacrificed the lives and future of all the citizens and of the nation.

Based on these considerations and because of the mounting public pressure, the head of state Ólafur Ragnar Grímsson refused to ratify the nationalization law wanted by Prime Minister Geir Haarde and called for a referendum.

The international community increased the pressure on Iceland. Great Britain and Holland threatened dire reprisals that would isolate the country. As Icelanders went to vote, foreign bankers threatened to block any aid from the IMF. The British government threatened to freeze Icelander's savings and deposit accounts.

As Grímsson said:

"We were told that if we refused the international community's conditions, we would become the Cuba of the North. But if we had accepted, we would have become the Haiti of the North."

In the March 2010 referendum, 93% of the population voted against repaying the debt. The IMF immediately froze its loan. But the revolution (though not televised in the United States and in Europe), would not be intimidated. With the support of a furious citizenry, the government launched civil and penal investigations into those responsible for the financial crisis. Interpol put out an international arrest warrant for the ex-president of Kaupthing, Sigurdur Einarsson, as the other bankers implicated in the crash fled the country. A total of about 5 thousand people left the island.

But Icelanders didn't stop there: they decided to draft a new constitution that would free the country from the exaggerated power of international finance. To write the new constitution, the people of Iceland elected twenty-five citizens from among 522 adults not belonging to any political party but recommended by at least thirty citizens. This document was not the work of a handful of politicians, but was written on the internet. The constituent's meetings were streamed on-line, and citizens could send their comments and suggestions, witnessing the document as it took shape. The way in which the new constitution was drafted was the real innovation, which overturned the notion that the foundations of a nation are dictated by few wise men.

The results speak for themselves. Iceland is growing by almost 5% with unemployment below 3% and ranks 6th in the United Nations Human Development Index and 4th in terms of per capita productivity.

Iceland is recovering from this terrible economic crisis and is performing in a way opposite to what is usually said to be inevitable in these situations.

No bailouts by the IMF, ECB or EU, no sale of popular sovereignty to financial institutions, but rather a process of appropriation of the rights of participation.

In contrast, European countries following the International Monetary Fund and the European Central Bank measures show an increase in unemployment and depressed productivity. In Greece, unemployment is now 22% and in Spain 18% and is expected to increase due to the contraction of the economy.

The figures are staggering, and Iceland shows that the nation that strongly opposed the blackmail of the financial institutions, which has reaffirmed the principle of popular sovereignty by refusing to pay the debt which was contracted by private bankers and unscrupulous and unethical brokers, is also the county which is performing better after the terrible financial crisis that started in 2008.

The financial elite of the world said that Iceland was going to be the Cuba of the North and condemned the country to a fate of extreme poverty, if its citizens did not follow what IMF and ECB dictated. But Icelanders with two referendums and with a plebiscitary result argued that private debts cannot be nationalized. The facts proved that Icelanders were right and that IMF and ECB were not looking after the interests of the citizens.

The people of Iceland have shown that representative democracy can be changed into participatory democracy and have started what they call a "*silent revolution*".

They now have a new constitution, drafted by an assembly democratically elected with the help of internet and the continuous involvement of citizens. Some towns, including the capital Reykjavik, now have online platforms for direct democracy, seeking to increasingly involve citizens in the decision making process of the government, in a virtuous cycle of social participation.

Iceland reaffirmed the basic principle that it is the will of the sovereign people which determines the welfare and the destiny of a nation. Iceland has shown how a nation can reaffirm the principle of the sovereign of the will of the people, which must prevail over the claims of any international financial institution.

- The debt scam and representative democracy

During the Bretton Woods meeting the victory of the US position and of the conditions that made the FED the most important institution of the new monetary system, implied several other important facts which soon shaped the new world order. Probably the most important one has to do with representative democracy.

No one can disapprove the commitment of the US to free the world from dictators and establish democracies everywhere. But let us see more into what this implies.

The word democracy was coined in Athens in 507 BC, combining the words *demos* (people) and *kratos* (power) and means that the power is in the hands of the people. Greek democracy was direct and it allowed all citizens to participate, speak and vote in the legislative assemblies.

Conversely we now use the word democracy to mean something different.

With democracy we denote a system that is based on the election of people's representatives. These representatives have the power to elect other representatives. In many countries they elect the president or the prime minister.

Yet few representatives have the financial resources to get elected. For example in the 2016 US Presidential campaign Hillary Clinton raised $1.4 billion and spent most of it for the campaign.

It is self-evident that ordinary people are not able to raise this amount of money and if they would be able to they would not be supported by the establishment (the FED) and they would be denied the access to the Main Stream Media (MSM).

In the 2016 US Presidential election, a President was elected without the support of the FED. Donald Trump managed to win the 2016 US Presidential elections without receiving any financial support by the establishment and the main stream media. It is quite natural that the establishment got into panic when Trump was elected and started a fierce campaign against him.

In 1911 Robert Michels wrote the book *"Political Parties, A Sociological Study of the Oligarchical Tendencies of Modern Democracy."*[10]

He shows that the costs of electoral campaigns and the organization of the party have transformed representative democracies into the dictatorship of a small elite, which pursues aims which differ and are in conflict

---

[10] socserv.mcmaster.ca/econ/ugcm/3ll3/michels/polipart.pdf

with the interests of the people and the country.

An example was provided by Adolf Hitler. Thanks to financial and media support, he gained 11 million votes in the 1932 elections, and this allowed him to become Chancellor.

According to Michels the function of representative democracy is to put servants of the private central banks (the establishment) in key positions.

These politicians inevitably end increasing the public debt and work for the hegemonic interests of the few that own the central banks.

- Comments

The plan of concentrating incredible quantities of wealth and resources is harming humanity as a whole and has no chances to succeed.

The reason is quite simple, we can observe two tendencies in energy one is diverging and dissipative (entropy) and one is converging and absorbing (syntropy).

Accumulating resources and wealth through private central banks increases entropy (i.e. wars, crises and illnesses) which inevitably leads to thermal death and the destruction of life.

The elite chosen to take humanity to the next interglacial period will live in well-designed shelters. An example is provided by fallout shelters in Switzerland such as the *Sonnenberg Tunnel* which is a modest version of what is needed to "ferry" the chosen elite to the next interglacial period. Parallel to this we have the *Svalbard Global Seed Vault* which is a secure seed bank on the Norwegian island of Spitsbergen near Longyearbyen in the remote Arctic Svalbard archipelago, designed to preserve a wide variety of plant seeds.

The transition of the chosen elite into the shelters should have taken place in the late 2016, just after the US presidential elections.

Before the US presidential elections took place in November 2016 the tension with Russia was mounting, NATO had encircled Russia and was conducting drills right on the border of Russia, contravening the international laws which require that drills must take place at least 20 kilometers away from the border.

Provocations were continuous and troops and weapons of mass destruction, such as nuclear warheads, were amassed on the borders with Russia. Clinton was pro-war whereas Trump was against the war. If Clinton had won, war with Russia would have started in a matter of days and by Spring 2017 the Third World War would have been raging and the transfer into the shelters would have taken place.

The rest of humanity would have perished under the fallout of the massive nuclear attacks.

But, something went wrong. When the polls closed everyone was sure Clinton was going to win. Trump himself did not believe he could win. Bettors were giving a 95% chance to Clinton and less than 5% to Trump. When Trump won Clinton's reaction was that the elections had been hacked by the Russians.

Donald Trump was the first president to win the presidential election without receiving any support from the *System* (the FED). It is only natural that the *System* panicked and started a fierce denigration campaign against Trump, accusing him of being a Russian agent at Putin's service, a traitor.

The Russiagate, the judicial investigation born as a result of the suspected interference by Russia in the 2016 presidential election, and conducted by special prosecutor Robert Mueller, showed that there was no interference, and made it clear the aberrant overwhelming power of the *System*.

Trump, probably unaware of it, winning the elections provided a chance to the third scenario in which the incoming ice-age will be faced by a united humanity.

SCENARIO #3:
HUMANITY AS A WHOLE

Life constantly demonstrates the existence of a law opposite to entropy which is here named *syntropy* from the combination of the Greek words *syn* which means converging and *tropos* which means tendency.

While the second scenario is based on the law of entropy which is the tendency towards energy dissipation and thermal death, the third scenario is based on the law of syntropy which is the tendency towards energy concentration and the increase in temperatures.

Erwin Schrödinger[11] answering the question of what allows life to counter entropy, wrote: [12]

"It feeds on negative entropy. It is by avoiding the

---

[11] Erwin Schrödinger (1887–1961) was a Nobel Prize-winning Austrian physicist.
[12] Schrödinger E. (1944), *What is life?*
http://whatislife.stanford.edu/LoCo_files/What-is-Life.pdf

rapid decay into the inert state of 'equilibrium' that an organism appears so enigmatic; so much so, that from the earliest times of human thought some special non-physical or supernatural force (vis viva, entelechy) was claimed to be operative in the organism, and in some quarters is still claimed."

The same conclusion was reached by Albert Szent-Györgyi.[13]

"It is impossible to explain the qualities of organization and order of living systems starting from the entropic laws of the macrocosm. This is one of the paradoxes of modern biology: the properties of living systems are opposed to the law of entropy that governs the macrocosm."[14]

Györgyi continues:

"A major difference between amoebas and humans

---

[13] Albert Szent-Györgyi (1893–1986) was a Hungarian biochemist who won the Nobel Prize in Physiology or Medicine in 1937. He first isolated vitamin C and discoved the components and reactions of the citric acid cycle.
[14] Szent-Györgyi A. (1977), *Drive in Living Matter to Perfect Itself*, Synthesis 1, Vol. 1, No. 1, 14-26.

is the increase of complexity that requires the existence of a mechanism that is able to counteract the law of entropy. In other words, there must be a force that is able to counter the universal tendency of matter towards chaos and energy towards dissipation. Life always shows a decrease in entropy and an increase in complexity, in direct conflict with the law of entropy."

The main problem, according to Györgyi, is that:

"We see a profound difference between organic and inorganic systems ... as a scientist I cannot believe that the laws of physics become invalid as soon as you enter the living systems. The law of entropy does not govern living systems."

Other scientists suggest the need of a law symmetric to entropy. The paleontologist Teilhard de Chardin[15] pointed out that:

"Reduced to its essence, the problem of life can be

---

[15] Pierre Teilhard de Chardin (1881–1955) was a French paleontologist and geologist and Jesuit priest who conceived the idea of the Omega Point.

expressed as follows: once we admit the two major Laws of Energy Conservation and of Entropy (to which physics is limited), how can we add, without contradictions, a third universal law (which is expressed by biology) ... The situation is clarified when we consider at the basis of cosmology the existence of a second kind of entropy (or anti-entropy)."

- *Syntropy*

The notion of energy comes from the fact that physical systems possess a quantity that can be turned into a force.

This quantity can take the form of heat, mass, electromagnetism, potential, kinetic, nuclear and chemical energy.

Despite the fact that it is used and studied:

"it is important to realize that in physics today we have no knowledge of what energy is."[16]

---

[16] Feynman R (1965), *The Feynman Lectures on Physics*, California Institute of Technology, 1965, 3.

The energy-mass relation:

$$E = mc^2$$

that we all associate with Einstein, was first published by Oliver Heaviside in 1890[17], then by Henri Poincaré in 1900[18] and by Olinto De Pretto in 1904[19]. Olinto De Pretto presented it at the *Reale Istituto Veneto di Scienze* in an essay with a preface by the astronomer and senator Giovanni Schiaparelli.

It seems that this equation has come to Einstein through his father Hermann who was responsible for the lighting systems in Verona and who, as director of the *"Privilegiata Impresa Elettrica Einstein"*, had frequent contacts with the Fonderia De Pretto that produced the turbines for electricity.

However, the $E=mc^2$ does not take into account the momentum, which is also a form of energy and in 1905 Einstein added the

[17]Auffray J.P., *Dual origin of E=mc2*:http://arxiv.org/pdf/physics/0608289.pdf
[18]Poincaré H,. *Arch. néerland. sci.* 2, 5, 252-278 (1900).
[19]De Pretto O., *Lettere ed Arti*, LXIII, II, 439-500 (1904), Reale Istituto Veneto di Scienze.

momentum (p), thus obtaining the energy-momentum-mass equation:

$$E^2 = m^2 c^4 + p^2 c^2$$

Since energy is squared (E^2) and in the momentum (p) there is time a square root is used and there are two solutions: negative time energy and positive time energy.

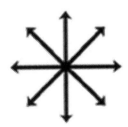

E^{-t}, negative time energy, manifests as converging energy   *E^{+t}, positive time energy, manifests as diverging energy*

Positive time energy implies causality, whereas negative time energy implies retrocausality: the future that acts back into the past. This was considered impossible and to solve this paradox Einstein removed the momentum, given the fact that it is practically equal to zero compared to the speed of light (c). In this way, he returned to the $E=mc^2$.

However, in 1924 the spin of the electron was discovered. The spin is an angular momentum, a rotation of the electron on itself at a speed close to that of light. Since this speed is very high, the momentum cannot be considered equal to zero and in quantum mechanics the energy-momentum-mass equation must be used with its uncomfortable dual solution.

The first equation that combined relativity and quantum mechanics was formulated in 1926 by Oskar Klein and Walter Gordon and has two time solutions: advanced and delayed waves. Advanced waves were rejected, since they imply retrocausality which was considered impossible.

The second equation, formulated in 1928 by Paul Dirac, also has two time solutions: electrons and neg-electrons (now called positron). The existence of positrons was proved in 1932 by Carl Andersen.

Shortly after Wolfgang Pauli and Carl Gustav Jung formulated the theory of synchronicities. Starting from the dual time solution of energy they came to the conclusion that reality is supercausal, with causes acting from the past and synchronicities acting from the future.

In 1933 Heisenberg, who had a strong charismatic personality and a leading position in the institutions and academia, declared the backward in time solution impossible. From that moment, anyone who ventures into the study of the backward in time solution is discredited, loses the academic position, the ability to publish and to talk at conferences.

Luigi Fantappiè studied pure mathematics at the Normale di Pisa, the most exclusive Italian University, where he had been classmate of Enrico Fermi. He was well known and appreciated among physicists to the point that in 1951 Oppenheimer invited him to become a member of the exclusive Institute for Advanced Study in Princeton and work directly with Einstein.

As a mathematician Fantappiè could not accept that Heisenberg had rejected half of the solutions of the fundamental equations and in 1941, while listing the properties of the forward and backward in time energy, Fantappiè discovered that the forward in time energy is governed by the law of *entropy*, whereas the backward in time energy is governed by a complementary law that he named *syntropy*, combining the Greek words *syn* which means converging and *tropos* which means tendency.

Entropy is the tendency towards energy dissipation, the famous second law of thermodynamics, also known as the law of heat death. On the contrary, syntropy is the tendency towards energy concentration, increase in differentiation, complexity and structures. These are the mysterious properties of life!

In 1944 Fantappiè published the book *"Principi di una Teoria Unitaria del Mondo Fisico e Biologico"* (Unitary Theory of the Physical and Biological World) in which he suggests that the physical-material world is governed by entropy and causality, while the biological world is governed by syntropy and retrocausality.[20]

We cannot see the future and therefore retrocausality is invisible! The dual energy solution suggests the presence of a visible reality (causal and entropic) and an invisible one (retrocausal and syntropic).

The first law of thermodynamics states that energy is a unity that cannot be created or destroyed, but only transformed, and the energy-momentum-mass equation shows that this unity has two components: entropy and syntropy. We can therefore write:

$$1 = Entropy + Syntropy \qquad Syntropy = 1 - Entropy$$

where syntropy is the complement of entropy! Life lies in-between these two components: one visible and the other invisible, one entropic and the other syntropic, and this can be described using a seesaw.

---

[20] Fantappiè L., *Principi di una teoria unitaria del mondo fisico e biologico*. Humanitas Nova, Roma 1944.

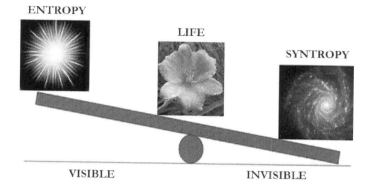

ENTROPY

LIFE

SYNTROPY

VISIBLE   INVISIBLE

We cannot see the future and therefore syntropy is invisible!

An example is provided by gravity. We continually experience gravity, but we cannot see it. According to the dual time energy solution gravity is a force that diverges backwards in time and, for us moving forward in time, it is a converging force. The fact that gravity is invisible is known to all, but that it diverges from the future is known to few.

Can we prove it?

Yes, and it's quite simple. If gravity propagates from the future its speed must exceed that of light. Tom van Flandern[21] developed a series of procedures to measure the speed of gravity propagation.[22,23,24]

In the case of light, which has a constant speed of about 300,000 kilometers per second, we observe the phenomenon of aberration. Sunlight takes about 500 seconds to reach the Earth. So when it arrives, we see the Sun in the sky position it occupied 500 seconds before. This difference is equivalent to about 20 seconds of arc, a large amount for astronomers. Sunlight strikes the Earth from a slightly shifted angle and this shift is called aberration.

If the speed of gravity propagation were limited, one would expect to observe aberration in gravity measurements. Gravity should be maximum in the position occupied

---

[21] Thomas Van Flandern (1940–2009) was an American astronomer and author specializing in celestial mechanics with a career as a professional scientist.
[22] Van Flander T. (1996), *Possible New Properties of Gravity*, Astrophysics and Space Science 244:249-261.
[23] Van Flander T. (1998), *The Speed of Gravity What the Experiments Say*, Physics Letters A 250:1-11.
[24] Van Flandern T. and Vigier J.P. (1999), *The Speed of Gravity – Repeal of the Speed Limit*, Foundations of Physics 32:1031-1068.

by the Sun when gravity left the Sun. Instead, observations indicate that there is no detectable delay in the propagation of gravity from the Sun to the Earth. The direction of the gravitational attraction of the Sun is exactly towards the position in which the Sun is, not towards a previous position, and this shows that the speed of propagation of gravity is infinite.

Instant propagation of gravity can only be explained if we accept that gravity is a force that diverges backwards in time, a physical manifestations of syntropy.

Fantappiè failed to prove his theory, since the experimental method requires the manipulation of causes before observing their effects.

Recently, random event generators (REG) have become available. These systems allow to perform experiments in which causes are manipulated after their effects: in the future.

The first experimental study on retrocausality, by Dean Radin of ION

(Institute of Noetic Sciences)[25], measured heart rate, skin conductance and blood pressure in subjects who were presented with blank images for 5 seconds followed by images that, based on a random event generator, could be neutral or emotional. The results showed a significant activation of the parameters of the autonomic nervous system, before the presentation of emotional images.

In 2003, Spottiswoode and May, of the Cognitive Science Laboratory, replicated this experiment by performing a series of controls to study possible artifacts and alternative explanations. The results confirmed those already obtained by Radin[26]. Similar results were obtained by other authors, such as McCraty, Atkinson and Bradley[27], Radin and

---

[25] Radin D.I. (1997), *Unconscious perception of future emotions: An experiment in presentiment*, Journal of Scientific Exploration, 11(2): 163-180.
[26] Spottiswoode P (2003) e May E, *Skin Conductance Prestimulus Response: Analyses, Artifacts and a Pilot Study*, Journal of Scientific Exploration, 2003, 17(4): 617-641.
[27] McCratly R (2004), Atkinson M e Bradely RT, *Electrophysiological Evidence of Intuition: Part 1*, Journal of Alternative and Complementary Medicine; 2004, 10(1): 133-143.

Schlitz[28] and May, Paulinyi and Vassy[29], always using the parameters of the autonomic nervous system.

Daryl Bem, psychologist and professor at the Cornell University, describes nine classic experiments conducted in the retrocausal mode in order to get the effects first rather than after the stimulus. For example, in a priming experiment, the subject is asked to judge whether the image is positive (pleasant) or negative (unpleasant) by pressing a button as quickly as possible. The reaction time is recorded.[30]

Just before the positive or negative image, a word is presented briefly, below the threshold so that it is not perceptible at a conscious level. This word is called *"prime"* and it has been

---

[28] Radin DI (2005) e Schlitz MJ, *Gut feelings, intuition, and emotions: An exploratory study*, Journal of Alternative and Complementary Medicine, 2005, 11(4): 85-91.
[29] May EC (2005), Paulinyi T e Vassy Z, *Anomalous Anticipatory Skin Conductance Response to Acoustic Stimuli: Experimental Results and Speculation about a Mechanism*, The Journal of Alternative and Complementary Medicine. August 2005, 11(4): 695-702.
[30] Bem D (2011), *Feeling the future: Experimental evidence for anomalous retroactive influences on cognition and affect*, Journal of Personality and Social Psychology, Jan 31, 2011.

observed that subjects tend to respond more quickly when the prime is congruent with the following image, whether it is a positive or negative image, while the reactions become slower when they are not congruent, for example when the word is positive while the image is negative.

In retro-priming experiments, the usual stimulus procedure takes place later, rather than before the subject responds, based on the hypothesis that this "inverse" procedure can retrocausally influence the answers. The experiments were conducted on more than a thousand subjects and showed retrocausal effects with statistical significance of one possibility on 134,000,000,000 of being mistaken when affirming the existence of the retrocausal effect.

Syntropy explains these results in the following way:

"Since life feeds on syntropy, and syntropy flows backward in time, the parameters of the autonomic

nervous system that support vital functions must react in advance to future stimuli."

As part of her doctoral thesis in cognitive psychology, Antonella Vannini conducted four experiments using heart rate measurements to study the retrocausal effect.[31]

Each experimental trial was divided into 3 phases:

– *Phase 1,* in which 4 colors were displayed one after the other on the computer screen. The subject had to look at these colors and during their presentation the heart rate was measured.

---

[31] Vannini A., Retrocausality, experiments and theory, www.amazon.com/dp/B005JIN51O

- *Phase 2,* in which an image with 4 colored bars was displayed and the subject had to try to guess the color that the computer would have selected.
- *Phase 3,* in which the computer randomly selected the color and showed it full screen.

The hypothesis was that in the case of a retrocausal effect differences should be observed among the heart rates measured in phase 1 in correlation with the target color selected in phase 3 from the computer.

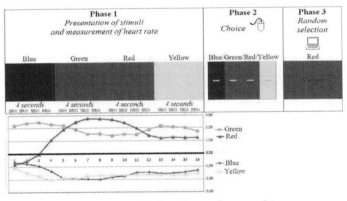

Retrocausal effect observed on a subject

In the absence of the retrocausal effect, the heart rates differences associated with each

color of the target stimulus should have varied around the zero value (0). Instead, a marked difference was observed!

Now a question arises:

"if syntropy is available at the quantum level how does it flow from the quantum level of matter to the macroscopic level of our physical reality, transforming inorganic into organic matter?"

In 1925 Wolfgang Pauli discovered the hydrogen bond. In water molecules hydrogen atoms are in an intermediate position between the subatomic (quantum) and molecular (macrocosm) levels and provide a bridge that allows syntropy (cohesive forces) to flow from the micro to the macro. Hydrogen bonds increase cohesive forces (syntropy) and make water different from all other liquids. Because of these cohesive forces ten times stronger than the van der Waals forces that hold the other liquids together, water shows abnormal properties. For example, when it solidifies it expands and floats; on the contrary, other liquids become denser, heavier and sink. The uniqueness of water stems from the cohesive properties of syntropy that allow the construction of networks and structures on a large scale.

Hydrogen bonds let syntropy flow from the subatomic level to the macrocosm level, making water essential for life. Ultimately, water is the lifeblood, the essential element for the manifestation and evolution of any biological structure. Other peculiarities of water are: [32]

— In liquids the solidification process starts from the bottom, as the hot molecules move upwards, while the cold molecules move downwards. The liquid in the lower part is therefore the first that reaches the solidification temperature; for this reason the liquids solidify starting from the bottom. In the case of water, the opposite is true: water solidifies from the top.

---

[32] Ball P., H_2O. *A biography of water,* www.amazon.it/dp/0753810921

- Water has a much higher thermal capacity than other liquids. Water can absorb large amounts of heat, then released slowly. The amount of heat needed to raise water temperature is far greater than that required for other liquids.
- When cold water is compressed it becomes more fluid. In contrast, in other liquids the viscosity increases with pressure.
- Friction between the surfaces of solids is usually high, while with ice friction is low and ice surfaces are slippery.
- At temperatures close to freezing, ice surfaces stick together when they come into contact. This mechanism allows snow to compact into snowballs, while it is impossible to produce balls of flour, sugar or other solid materials if you do not use water.
- With water the distance between the melting and the boiling temperatures is very high. Water molecules have high cohesive properties that increase the temperature needed to change water from liquid to gas.

Water is not the only molecule with hydrogen bonds. Also ammonia and hydrofluoric acid form hydrogen bonds and these molecules show anomalous properties similar to water. However, water produces a higher number of hydrogen bonds and this determines the high cohesive properties of water that bind the molecules into large and dynamic labyrinths.

Other molecules forming hydrogen bonds fail to construct complex networks and structures in space. Hydrogen bonds impose extremely unusual structural constraints for a liquid. An example of these constraints is provided by snow crystals. However, when water freezes, the mechanism of the hydrogen bond stops and the flow of syntropy from the micro to the macro also stops, bringing life to death.

Hydrogen bonds make water essential for life, water provides syntropy to living systems. If life ever starts on another planet, surely water would be needed. Water is the only means by which life draws syntropy from the quantum level. Consequently, it is indispensable for the origin and evolution of any biological structure.

Hydrogen bonds impose structural constraints that are extremely unusual for a liquid, and these in turn affect physical properties such as density, heat capacity and heat conduction, as well as the way water receives within it solute molecules.

When water is super cooled to the experimental limit of -38°C, its thermal capacity increases considerably. At the theoretical limit of -45°C the thermal capacity of water becomes infinite; water could absorb infinite amounts of heat without increasing in temperature. At this theoretical limit, even the slightest increase in pressure would make water disappear, similarly to what happens with black holes in which temporal inversion makes matter disappear.

The syntropic properties of water suggest that water is constantly under the effect of retrocausal forces. This would explain why it is so difficult to predict the behavior of water molecules even in a small glass.

Based on these considerations, in February 2011 with Antonella Vannini I wrote an article for the Journal of Cosmology commenting on an article by dr. Richard Hoover[33] of NASA Marshall Space Flight Center.

Dr. Hoover discovered microfossils, similar to cyanobacteria, in internal sections of comet meteorites and, using electron microscopy and a series of other measures, concluded that they originated from these meteors, ie comets.

According to syntropy, life is a general law of the universe which requires the presence of water to manifest itself. A characteristic of comets is that they are rich in ice which, in the vicinity of the Sun, melts and becomes water; therefore in our article[34] we suggested that, according to syntropy, living organisms can originate in extreme conditions, such as those of comets, and that the discovery of Dr. Hoover of cyanobacteria microfossils in

---

[33] Hoover R (2001), *Fossils of Cyanobacteria in CI1 Carbonaceous Meteorites, Journal of Cosmology*, 2011, http://journalofcosmology.com/Life100.html
[34] Vannini A (2011) and Di Corpo U, *Extraterrestrial Life, Syntropy and Water*, Journal of Cosmology, http://journalofcosmology.com/Life101.html#18

meteorites is consistent with the theory of syntropy.

- *Comments*

In order for life to survive it is necessary to:

— have liquid water;
— reduce entropy and increase syntropy.

We need liquid water since the hydrogen bond does not work with ice. This means that heat and the access to energy are vital requirements.

It is important to note that most of the energy that we use comes from wood, coal, petrol and gas, which have organic origins.

This shows that life absorbs energy and allows to increase temperatures. Therefore, in order to contrast the cooling effect of the ice-age we need to maximize life.

Life is syntropic, it is energy absorbing, it increases temperatures and produces CO_2. It is therefore fundamental to take full advantage of life in order to compete against the freezing effects of the ice-age.

For example deserts reflect heat and cool the planet, on the contrary forests absorb heat and warm the planet. It is therefore imperative to reduce deserts and increase forests. This is just one of the many examples. Deserts must be changed into forests as quickly as possible in order to reduce the cooling of the planet.

Strangely, this process of afforestation will be helped by the ice-age. Ice ages are unbelievably important for the planet since they provide a powerful water pumps. During ice ages rains increase and immense quantities of water fall on the land and stay in the form of ice and snow. Ice ages replenish the land with salt-free water suitable for life, creating the conditions which will turn the planet into a prosperous garden.

We don't have to wait for glacial temperatures, the ice age water pump is already active and we can use it to turn the planet into a great forest. We can start right away, exploiting this powerful water pump effect which is already showing in the form of extreme weather conditions.

During the interglacial warm periods water slowly dries out and temperatures increase causing desertification and the reduction of the ice caps. If we learn to take advantage of the ice-age cycles we can transform the planet into a permanent garden of Eden, an heaven on earth.

Ice-ages have an extremely positive effect on the planet, solving desertification, replenishing water resources and cleaning all which is damaging and toxic for life. Ice-ages are vital for life and we need to learn how to get advantage from them in order to promote a plentiful, beautiful and healthy life.

How can we allow the ice-age to fulfill its function and at the same time how can we survive as a civilized species.

The ice age increases rainfalls and this facilitate afforestation and the transformation of deserts. At the same time forests activate the "biotic pump" effect which brings vapor from the oceans to dry areas, such as deserts.

A green planet will absorb more energy and heat and this will reduce the cooling effect of the ice age.

Since life increases temperatures, in order to contrast the ice-age we need to increase life. As it will be shown later simulations suggest that a world population of over 100billion people will be needed to contrast the ice age. This might seems impossible, but this is the challenge we are heading to.

Before entering in the details of this third scenario it is necessary to provide some more information.

We will start discussing how we can lower entropy and increase syntropy at the individual level and how a syntropic monetary system should be organized. We will then start describing the third scenario.

HOW INDIVIDUALS CAN
INCREASE SYNTROPY

The complementarity between entropy and syntropy can be represented as a seesaw with causality on one side and retrocausality on the other side.

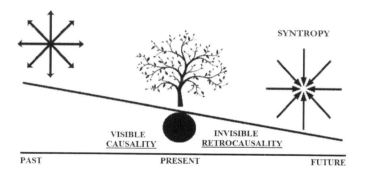

Life is the manifestation of syntropy and it constantly fights entropy. Since, our activities tend to increase entropy the challenge is:

how can we increase syntropy
and reduce entropy
by remaining active?

101

To describe this challenge I will start with the example of a freelance, single, whose expenses exceeded the income of over five hundred euros a month. The reader should focus on the key concepts and see how they can be extended to other situations.

In this example the savings were running out and this freelance had no one to ask for help. He started reducing his expenses: no money in his wallet, no credit on his mobile phone. But things were going from bad to worse. At this point he asked for help. Let's see how it went.

«*How much do you spend on your mobile phone?*»
«*About 40 euros a month, but I always find myself without credit.*»
«*Why don't you change provider? There are interesting promotions. With only 10 euros a month you can have unlimited minutes and SMS and 20 gigabytes of internet.*»

Lowering entropy means saving, but this must be done by maintaining or increasing the quality of life.

In this case, changing provider and choosing a new contract increases the quality of life and leads to save over three hundred euros a year!

The rule is to improve the quality of life by saving. The same logic can be applied to organizations, institutions and nations.

When entropy (expenses) and syntropy (incomes) are balanced, the invisible world begins to manifest in the form of synchronicities.

In this example we need to reduce spending by at least six thousand euros a year.

«Do you take shirts to the laundry to be ironed?»

«I wash them, but I am not able to iron them. I take them to the laundry to have them ironed.»

«How much does it cost you?»

«Between 50 and 70 euros a month.»

«Why don't you ask your maid if she can iron them for 8 euros more per month?»

The maid immediately accepted. Another small optimization that led to save but which significantly increased the quality of life by eliminating the hassle of going to the laundry.

Again an increase in the quality of life while saving!

Each situation and context is unique. The way how to increase the quality of life while saving can vary incredibly and consequently each approach must be tailored.

These first two optimizations have reduced entropy by around one thousand euros and increased the quality of life. The goal is to reach six thousand euros to balance income and expenses.

«Do you go to work by car?»

«I also use the scooter to save money, but the traffic is really dangerous!»

«Why don't you use your bicycle?»

«On these roads ?!»

«No, on alternative roads.»

«My house is in the city center, the office is not far away, but I have always considered the bicycle impossible due to the difference in altitude of over 30 meters. I would arrive tired and sweaty.»

«If you have to climb it is better to choose a steep but short road, get off and push, rather than pedaling.»

Thus he discovered the beauty of the streets of the city center and parks. In less than 25 minutes he could reach his office by bicycle. It took more time by car or scooter. The next day he sold the scooter, canceled the insurance and the garage. Another three thousand euros saved per year. With this simple optimization, he has received other advantages: he exercises and no longer needs to go to the gym, more money and time saved! Moreover, he spends less on fuel.

Entropy has now decreased by over four thousand euros a year and the quality of life has improved!

We need to find another two thousand euros before the invisible world can begin to show.

«*Your electricity bill exceeds 200 euros every two months! As a single you should not pay more than 50 euros.*»

«*What should I do?*»

«*Try using low energy light bulbs, such as LED lamps, and set the timer to the water heater.*»

Small changes that required little time and

money. One hundred and fifty euros saved every two months, nine hundred euros a year. <u>With this small optimization he felt consistent with his ecological beliefs and the quality of life increased</u>. Now he had reduced his expenses by over five thousand euros a year! We must reach the goal of six thousand euros a year!

«How much do you pay for electricity in your office?»
«About 300 euros every two months.»
«Do you use halogen spotlights !?»
«Yes.»

He discovered that he could save over a thousand euros a year simply by replacing the halogen spotlights with LED spotlights.

<u>Now that expenses no longer exceed the incomes, syntropy can begin to show in the form of synchronicities</u>.

Jung and Pauli have coined the term synchronicity to indicate an invisible causality different from that familiar to us. Synchronicities manifest as meaningful coincidences, because they converge towards an end.

Invisible causality acts from the future and groups events according to purpose. Synchronicities are significant because they have a purpose.

«How much do you pay for renting your office?»
«Nothing. It is owned by my aunts.»
«They could rent it and make a profit, but you use it for free ?!»
«Exactly.»
«And what are your aunts living on?»
«They both receive a pension and have some savings, but their financial situation is not good, they constantly complain.»
«Have you ever thought about renting a room in an office and letting your aunts rent their apartment?»
«I have no money, I can't afford to pay a rent!»
«How's your business going?»
«I have few clients, perhaps because of the economic crisis, but also because of the position of the office.»
«A less prestigious office, but in a strategic and well-connected place could help you have more customers ?!»

The first synchronicity is the following. The day after this dialogue, as if by magic, he received the offer of a room in an office in the most central area of the city, at the price of only 250 euros a month, including all utilities! The aunts' apartment was in a very beautiful and prestigious place, but difficult to reach and there was no parking: beautiful, prestigious, but inconvenient and very expensive. However he hesitated, he didn't dare!

The next day another synchronicity occurred. He received a call from the doorkeeper. An airline offered 2,800 euros a month for his aunts' apartment. Obviously the aunts asked him to find another place immediately and fortunately the day before he had received the offer of a room. But he still wasn't convinced. The office in the city center was in a very noisy area: well connected, but chaotic.

The third synchronicity is the following. That same afternoon he was walking in the area of the city he likes most. It is not central, but it is green, quiet and well connected. At a shoemaker's window, he saw a notice for a room in an office. The apartment was in the building next to the shoemaker. He called and immediately went to see it. He instantly decided to rent the room. In a city like Rome it is difficult to find rooms for rent in professional studios and above all in such a beautiful place of the city.

When synchronicities show, we are attracted to places and situations that otherwise we would not take into consideration and that solve our problems. Synchronicities are accompanied by feelings of warmth and well-being in the thoracic area that inform us that we are on the right path.

«*I began to feel warmth and well-being in the chest area. My clients like the new studio. There is parking place, it is nice, quiet and it is located near a metro station. My business is thriving, my savings are increasing and my personal and sentimental life has improved.*»

<u>Syntropy offers wealth and happiness. But when things go well it is easy to fall back into the old entropic lifestyles.</u>
A few months later he received a job offer, a prestigious job abroad: his dream!

He immediately accepted and moved. The salary was high, taxation was low. Suddenly he would become a rich man who could lead the rich life he had always wanted.

But this reverses the balance between entropy and syntropy: <u>wealth leads to an entropic lifestyle: entropy increases and syntropy decreases and we fall back into the crisis</u>!

«The foreign company was only interested in making money, without any ethics. I had to work almost fifty hours a week, there was nothing else outside the company. It was necessary to give absolute priority to what was profitable, even if immoral. A few months later I felt disgusted with my profession. Taxes were low, but I had to pay all the services. By adding the rent of the house and the expenses related to the fact that I was a foreigner, I paid much more than I earned. After only six months I had accumulated more than twenty-eight thousand euros of debts! The dream had broken and had become a nightmare. From heaven I fell to hell. I had no time for myself or for my love life. First I felt discomfort, then suffering, and eventually depression and anxiety exploded. I decided to go back to Italy!»

When syntropy increases people easily fall back into entropic lifestyles. Syntropy must be paired with the awareness that we don't obtain happiness and fulfillment through material wealth. This is true not only for individuals, but also for companies, institutions and nations.

The increase of syntropy, must always be accompanied by an inner transformation.

We will now try to sketch some elements of this inner transformation.

The mathematician Chris King suggests that we are constantly faced with bifurcations between information arriving from the past (*entropy*) and in-formation arriving from the future (*syntropy*).

Supercausal model of free will

These bifurcations entail choices and choosing forces us in a condition of free will.

Since the forward and the backward in time energy solutions are perfectly balanced, similar amounts of information (past) and in-formation (future) are received.

This might explain the perfect division of the brain in two hemispheres.

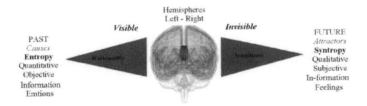

Where the left hemisphere is the seat of the "forward in time" logical reasoning and the right hemisphere is the seat of the "backward in time" intuitive reasoning.

The description of two complementary tendencies, one diverging from the past and one converging towards the future, one visible and one invisible, one destructive and one constructive, can be found in many philosophies and religions.

Carl Gustav Jung and Wolfgang Pauli added to causality (entropy) synchronicities (syntropy). According to Jung, synchronicities are experienced when two or more events which are unrelated are experienced as happening together in a meaningful way.

The concept of synchronicity does not question, or compete with, the notion of causality. Instead, it maintains that just as events may be grouped by causes, they may also be grouped by finalities, a meaningful principle.

Jung coined the word synchronicities to describe what he called *"temporally coincident occurrences of acausal events."*

He variously described synchronicity as an *"acausal connecting principle," "meaningful coincidence"* and *"acausal parallelism."*

Jung gave a full statement of this concept in the paper *Synchronicity - An Acausal Connecting Principle*,[35] jointly with a related study by the physicist Wolfgang Pauli.

---

[35] Jung C.G. (1951), *Synchronicity - An Acausal Connecting Principle*, Princeton University Press, www.amazon.com/dp/0691150508

In Jung's and Pauli's description causality acts from the past, whereas synchronicities act from the future. Synchronicities are meaningful since they lead towards a finality, providing a direction to events.

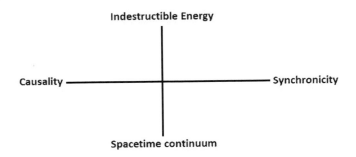

Jung and Pauli described causality and synchronicities acting on the same indestructible energy. They are united by this energy, but at the same time they are complementary.

In the Taoist philosophy all aspects of the universe are described as the interplay of two complementary and fundamental forces: the yang principle which is diverging, and the yin principle which is converging.

These two forces are part of a unity. In the visible side of reality, when one increases the other decreases, but as a whole their balance remains unchanged. This law is masterfully represented in the Taijitu symbol, that is the union of these opposite forces, the yin and the yang, the diverging and converging forces whose combined actions move the universe in all its aspects: the sexes, seasons, day and night, life and death, full and empty, movement and repose, push and pull, dry and wet.

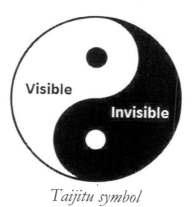

Taijitu symbol

In the Taijitu the yang principle is represented by the white color and has entropic properties, whereas the yin principle is represented by the black color and has syntropic properties.

The Taijitu is a wheel that rotates constantly,

changing the proportion of yin and yang (syntropy and entropy) in the visible and the invisible sides of reality.

The Taijitu shows that a property of complementarity is that opposites attract each other. This property is well known in physics, but it is also true at the human level where people on opposite polarities are attracted to each other, as in males and females. Since the balance of these opposite forces remains unchanged the Taoist philosophy suggests that the aim is to harmonize the opposites, thus creating unity.

In Hinduism the law of complementarity is described by the dance of Shiva and Shakti, where Shakti is the personification of the female principle and Shiva of the male principle. They represent the primordial cosmic energy and the dynamic forces that are thought to move through the entire universe. Shiva has the properties of syntropy, whereas Shakti has the properties of entropy and they are constantly combined together in an endless cosmic dance.

Shakti can never exist apart from Shiva or

act independently of him, just as Shiva remains a mere corpse without Shakti. All the matter and energy of the universe results from the dance of these two opposite forces. Shiva absorbs Shakti energy, turning it into a body, absolute pure consciousness, the light of knowledge. According to Hinduism intelligence comes from the future (Shiva), whereas fearsome, ferocity and aggressiveness come from the past (Shakti). Shakti is the energy of the physical and visible world whereas Shiva is the consciousness which transcends the visible world. However, each aspect of Shiva has a Shakti component. This endless dance between Shakti and Shiva has the function to bring life towards Unity.

Syntropy adds the autonomic nervous system (the heart).

The autonomic nervous system automatically and unconsciously regulates the vital functions of the body, without the need for any voluntary control. It provides visions of the future, insights, inspirations and higher levels of awareness, which are inaccessible to the ordinary states of the rational mind. It shows the direction, the goals and the mission of our life by acting as a teacher that guides us to the solution of problems and to well-being.

Almost all the visceral functions are under the control of the autonomic nervous system which is divided into the sympathetic and parasympathetic systems. The nerve fibers of these systems do not directly reach the organs, but stop first and form synapses with other neurons in structures called ganglia, from which other nerve fibers form systems, called plexuses, which reach the organs.

The sympathetic part of the system is close to the spinal ganglia and forms synapses together with longitudinal fibers, in a tree called the paravertebral chain. The parasympathetic system forms synapses away from the spine and closer to the organs it controls. The ganglia of the sympathetic system are distributed as follows: 3 pairs of intracranial ganglia, located along the trigeminal, 3 pairs of cervical ganglia connected to the heart; 12 pairs of dorsal ganglia connected to the lungs and the solar plexus, 4 pairs of lumbar ganglia that are connected through the solar plexus to the stomach, small intestine, liver, pancreas and kidneys, 4 pairs of ganglia in connection with the rectum, bladder and genital organs.

For a long time it was believed that there was no relationship between the brain and the sympathetic system, but today we know that this relationship exists, is strong and that the brain can act directly on the organs through the mediation of the solar plexus. There is therefore a link between mental states and physical states. For example, sadness acts on the solar plexus through the sympathetic system, generating a vasoconstriction due to the contraction of the arterial system. This contraction caused by sadness hinders blood circulation, thus also affecting digestion and respiration.

People commonly refer to the heart and not to the solar plexus. However, from a physiological point of view, the organ that allows us to perceive our inner feelings is the solar plexus.

Syntropy is energy that converges from the future and nourishes our vital functions. Consequently when the inflow of syntropy is good we feel warmth (ie energy concentration) and well-being.

On the contrary, when the inflow is insufficient we feel emptiness and pain (anxiety).

These feelings work like the needle of a compass which points towards the source of syntropy (the attractor).

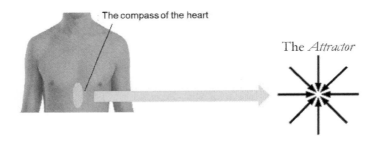

The compass of the heart

The *Attractor*

Unfortunately most people are unaware of this compass and their main concern is to avoid suffering and the unbearable feelings of anxiety.

This explains the mechanism of addiction.

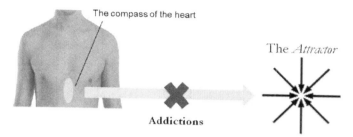

The compass of the heart

The *Attractor*

Addictions

Substances that act on the autonomic nervous system, such as alcohol and heroin, causing feelings of warmth and wellbeing similar to those that signal a good inflow of syntropy, can soon become vital.

The compass of the heart points to the attractor, but whatever we use to sedate our inner suffering reduces this perception.

In order to promote the inner transformation and wellbeing it is therefore essential to abandon any kind of addiction.

While the brain is made of gray matter outside and white matter inside, exactly the opposite happens in the solar plexus. The gray matter is made up of nerve cells that allow us to think, the white matter is made of nerve fibers that allow us to feel.

The solar plexus and the brain are the opposite of each other and represent two polarities: the emitter pole and the absorber pole. The same duality that is found between entropy and syntropy.

Experiments show that syntropy acts mainly on the solar plexus and is perceived as warmth and well-being. On the contrary, the lack of syntropy is perceived as emptiness and suffering.

Since syntropy propagates backwards in time, feelings of warmth and wellbeing help us orient our choices towards what is beneficial whereas feelings of void help us avoid what is dangerous.

For example:

— The article *"In Battle, Hunches Prove to be Valuable"*, published on the front page of the New York Times on July 28, 2009, describes intuitions and premonitions that helped soldiers save themselves: *"My body suddenly became cold; you know, that feeling of danger, and I started screaming no-no!"* Syntropy says that the attack happens causing fear which propagates backward in time. The soldier in the past feels this as a premonition and is driven to take a different decision, thus avoiding the attack and death. According to the New York Times article, premonitions have saved more lives than the billions of dollars spent on intelligence.

— William Cox, conducted studies on the number of tickets sold in the United States for commuter trains between 1950 and 1955 and found that for the 28 commuter trains that had accidents fewer tickets were sold[36]. Data analysis was repeated verifying all possible intervening variables, such as bad weather conditions, departure times, day of the week, etc. But no intervening variable explained the correlation between reduced ticket sales and accidents. The reduction of passengers on trains that have accidents is strong, not only from a statistical point of view, but also from a quantitative point of view. Syntropy

---

[36] Cox WE (1956), *Precognition: An analysis.* Journal of the American Society for Psychical Research, 1956(50): 99-109.

explains Cox's findings in this way: when people are involved in accidents feelings of pain and fear propagate backward in time and can be felt in the past in the form of presentiments and premonitions, which can lead to decide not to travel. This can change the past. A negative event occurs in the future and informs us in the past, through our feelings. Listening to our feelings can help to avoid pain and suffering in the future, changing it for the better.

— Among many possible examples: on May 22, 2010 an Air India Express Boeing 737-800 flying between Dubai and Mangalore crashed during landing, killing 158 passengers, only eight survived the accident. Nine passengers, after check-in, felt sick and could not get on board.

In this regard, the neurologist Antonio Damasio, who has studied people affected by decision-making deficits, discovered that feelings contribute to the decision-making process and make advantageous choices possible without having to make advantageous evaluations.[37]

Damasio observed that cognitive processes were added to emotional ones, maintaining the centrality of emotions in the decision-making process. This is evident in times of danger: when choices have to be quick reason is bypassed.

People with decision making deficit show knowledge but not feelings. Their cognitive functions are intact, but not the emotional ones. They have normal intellect, but are unable to make appropriate decisions. A dissociation between rationality and decision-making is observed. The alteration of feelings causes a myopia towards the future. This may be due to neurological lesions or to the use of substances, such as alcohol and heroin, which reduce the perception of our inner feelings.

Feelings of warmth point to the attractor and to what is beneficial to life. It is therefore good to choose according to these inner feelings.

Intuitions arise from the ability to feel and

---

[37] Damasio AR (1994), *Descarte's Error. Emotion, Reason, and the Human Brain*, Putnam Publishing, 1994.

are amplified when our feelings are not contaminated by drugs, alcohol and fears.

Henri Poincaré, one of the most intuitive mathematicians of the last century, observed that when faced with a new problem whose solutions can be countless, a rational approach is initially used, but being unable to arrive at the result another type of process is activated.

This process selects the correct solution among the endless possibilities, without the help of rationality.

Poincaré called it intuition (combining the Latin words *in*=inside + *tueri*=glance) since they are always accompanied by inner feelings of truth, warmth and well-being:[38]

"Among the large number of possible combinations, almost all are without interest or utility.
Only those that lead to solving the problem are illuminated by an interior experience of truth and beauty."

For Poincaré, intuitions require attention to

---

[38] Henri Poincaré, *Mathematical Creation*, from Science et méthode, 1908.

these inner feelings of truth and beauty, which connect us to the future, to the source of intelligence and creativity.

Robert Rosen (1934-1998), theoretical biologist and professor of biophysics at the Dalhousie University, in his book *Anticipatory Systems*[39] wrote:

"I was amazed by the number of anticipatory behaviors observed at all levels of the organization of living systems (...) that behave like real anticipatory systems, systems in which the present state changes according to future states, violating the law of causality according to which changes depend exclusively on past or present causes. We try to explain these behaviors with theories and models that exclude any possibility of anticipation. Without exception, all biological theories and models are classic in the sense that they seek only causes in the past or present."

To make anticipatory behaviors consistent with classical causality, predictive models are taken into account. But anticipatory behaviors

---

[39] Rosen R (1985) *Anticipatory Systems*, Pergamon Press, USA 1985.

are found also in the simpler forms of life, such as cells, without neural systems, and in these cases it is difficult to sustain the hypothesis of predictive models or learning processes. Furthermore, they are also observed in macromolecules and this excludes any possible explanation based on innate processes due to natural selection. Rosen concludes that a new law of causality is needed to explain the anticipatory behaviors of living systems.

The hypothesis that living systems use a different type of causality had been advanced by Hans Driesch (1867-1941), a pioneer in experimental research in embryology.

Driesch suggested the existence of final causes, which operate from the global to the analytic, from the future to the past. The final causes lead living matter to evolve towards the purpose of nature which Driesch called entelechies, from the Greek *en-telos* which means something that contains in itself its own purpose and that evolves towards this end. So, if the normal development path is interrupted, the system can reach the same end in another way. Driesch believed that the development and behavior of living systems were governed by a hierarchy of entelechies united by a single final entelechy.

Driesch provided the proof of this phenomenon by using sea urchin embryos. Dividing the sea urchin embryo cells after the first cell division, Driesch expected each cell to develop into the corresponding half of the animal for which it was designed or planned, but instead he discovered that each developed into a full sea urchin. This also happened in the four-cell stage: whole larvae developed from each of the four cells, although smaller than usual. It is possible to remove large pieces from the eggs, mix the blastomeres and interfere in many ways without affecting the embryo. It seems that every single monad in the original egg cell is able to form any part of the complete embryo. On the contrary, when two young embryos are joined, a single sea urchin is obtained and not two sea urchins.

These results show that sea urchins develop towards a morphological end. The moment we act on an embryo, the cell that survives continues to respond to the final cause that leads to the formation of structures. Although smaller, the structure that is reached is similar to the one that would have been obtained from the original embryo. It follows that the final form is not caused by the past or by a program, a project or a design that acts from the past, since any change we introduce in the past leads to the formation of the same structure. Even when a part of the system is removed or normal development is disturbed, the final form is reached which is always the same.

Another example is that of tissue regeneration. Driesch studied the process by which organisms are able to replace or repair damaged structures. Plants possess an extraordinary range of regenerative abilities, and the same happens with animals. For example, if a worm is cut into pieces, each piece regenerates a complete worm. Many vertebrates have an extraordinary capacity for regeneration, for example, if the lens of a newt's eye is surgically removed, a new lens is regenerated from the edge of the iris, while in the normal development of the embryo the lens is formed in a very different way, starting from the skin. Driesch used the concept of entelechy to explain the properties of integrity and directionality in the development and regeneration of living bodies and systems.

Independently in 1926 the Russian scientist Alexander Gurwitsch (1874-1954) and the Austrian biologist Paul Alfred Weiss (1898-1989) suggested the existence of a new causal factor, different from classical causality, which was called morphogenetic field. In addition to stating that morphogenetic fields play an important role in controlling morphogenesis (the development of body shape), the authors show that classical causality fails.

The term "field" is currently fashionable: gravitational field, electromagnetic field and morphogenetic field. It is used to indicate something that is observed, but is not yet understood in terms of classical causality; events that require a new type of explanation based on a new type of causality.

Syntropy replaces the terms "entelechies" and "fields" with the terms "final causes" and "attractors". Causes that act from the future produce fields that attract and guide.

Living systems are guided towards the future by intuitions, synchronicities and inner feelings that respond to attractors. The same happens in our lives:

Inner feelings guide us towards the attractor,
the purpose of our existence.

A very important example was provided by Steve Jobs, the founder of Apple Computer.

Steve Jobs had been abandoned by his natural parents and this was the drama that accompanied him throughout his life. He was tormented and never accepted being abandoned.

He left university during the first year and ventured to India where he discovered a completely different vision of the world:

"in the Indian countryside people do not let themselves be guided by rationality, as we do, but by intuitions."

He discovered that intuitions are very powerful. They are very developed in India, but practically unknown in the West.

He returned to the United States sure that intuitions are more powerful than rationality. Intuitions require a minimalist lifestyle and Jobs became vegan, no alcohol, tobacco or coffee, lots of meditation and the courage not to be influenced by the judgment of others.

His aim was to reduce entropy to the point that it took him more than 8 months to choose the washing machine. He absolutely had to find the one with the lowest energy consumption and maximum efficiency. He lived in a thrifty way, a life so essential and austere that led his children to believe he was poor.

The way he lived was the result of his need to focus on the inner feelings of the heart. He avoided wealth because it could distract from the voice of the heart. He was one of the richest men on the planet, but he lived a minimalist life! From a syntropic perspective, his minimalist choices allowed intuitions to emerge, becoming the source of his creativity and wealth.

Jobs believed that people don't know the future. Only intuitive people can feel it and bring it into the present.

When he returned from India he saw an electronic board at Steve Wozniak's house and he had the intuition of a computer that could be held in one hand. He asked Wozniak to develop a prototype of a personal computer, which he named Apple I. He managed to sell a few hundreds and this sudden success gave him the impetus to develop a more advanced model, suitable for ordinary people, which he named Apple II.

Jobs was not an engineer, he had no scientific or technical mind, he was simply an artist! What do computers have to do with his life? Jobs had nothing to do with electronics, but his intuitive abilities showed him a goal, an object of the future.

Thirty years earlier, in 1977, he intuited a pocket computer that combines aesthetics, simplicity, technology and minimalism! He felt the need for a product that, in addition to being technologically perfect, had to be also beautiful and simple!

His obsession with beauty and simplicity led him to devote an enormous amount of time to the details of the Apple II. It had to be beautiful, quiet and at the same time essential and simple!

It was an unprecedented commercial success that made Apple Computer one of the leading global companies.

Jobs noticed that when the heart gave him an intuition, it was a command he had to obey, regardless the opinions of others. The only thing that mattered was finding a way to give shape to the intuition.

For Jobs, the vegan diet, Zen meditation, a life immersed in nature, abstention from alcohol and coffee were necessary to nourish his inner voice, the voice of his heart and strengthen his ability to intuit the future.

At the same time, this caused great difficulties. He was sensitive, intuitive, irrational and emotional. He was aware of the limitations that his irrationality caused in handling a large company, such as Apple Computer, and chose a rationalist manager to run the company: John Sculley, a famous manager he admired but with whom he developed conflicts, to the point that in 1985 the board of directors decided to fire Jobs from Apple, the company he had founded.

Apple continued to make money with the products designed by Jobs, but after a few years the decline began and in the mid-1990s it came to the brink of bankruptcy. On December 21, 1996, the board of directors asked Jobs to return as the president's personal advisor. Jobs accepted. He asked for a salary of one dollar a year in exchange for the guarantee that his insights, even if crazy, were accepted unconditionally. In a few months he revolutionized the products and on September 16, 1997 he became interim CEO.

Apple Computer resurrected in less than a year. How did he manage?

He said we should not let the noise of others' opinions dull our inner voice. And, more importantly, he repeated that we must always have the courage to believe in our heart and in our intuitions, because they already know the future and know where we need to go. For Jobs, everything else was secondary.

Being interim has marked all his new products. Their name had to be preceded by the letter *i*: *i*Pod, *i*Pad, *i*Phone and *i*Mac.

Jobs' children believed he was poor. They often asked him: "*Daddy, why don't you take us to one of your rich friends?*"

He talked about important business walking in parks or in nature. To celebrate a success, he invited employees to restaurants for $10 per person. When he made a gift he collected flowers in a field. He wore the same clothes for years. Despite the immense riches he had!

He was convinced that money was not his, but that it was a tool to reach the end.

At the time of Apple I, he repeated that his mission was to develop a computer that could be held in one hand and not to get rich. For him money was exclusively a tool.

The ability to feel the future was the source of Jobs' wealth. It was the ingredient of his creativity, genius and innovation.

Einstein repeated that:

"*the intuitive mind is a sacred gift and the rational*

mind is its faithful servant. But we have created a society that honors the servant and has forgotten the gift."

Zen meditation helped Jobs calm his mind and move the attention to the heart.

In his lectures he used to say that almost everything, expectations, pride and fears of failure, vanish in the face of death. He emphasized the centrality of death and the fact that when we are aware of dying we pay attention only to what is really important. Being constantly aware that we are going to die is one of the most effective ways to focus on what is really important and to avoid the traps of materiality. We are already naked in the face of death. Since we must die, there is no reason not to follow our heart and do what we have to do.

Jobs believed in the invisible and in synchronicities. He built the headquarters of Pixar (one of his companies) around a central space, a large square where everyone had to go through if they wanted to eat something or use the services. In this way the invisible world was favored by chance encounters.

According to Jobs, chance does not exist. Chance encounters allow the invisible, to activate intuitions, creativity and synchronicities and make visible what is not yet visible.

Jobs loved to quote Michelangelo's famous phrase:

"In each block of marble I see a statue as if it were in front of me, shaped and perfect in attitude and action. I just have to remove the rough walls that imprison the beautiful appearance to reveal it to others as my eyes see it."

Jobs believed that we all have a task, a mission to carry out. We just need to discover this mission by removing all what is not necessary.

Jobs made visible what he had intuited. He died a few months after the presentation of the *i*Pad, the computer that can be held in one hand, the mission of his life.

The life of Jobs testifies that wealth and value come from the future and that the voice of the heart and intuitions bring the future into the present.

Now let's move on to another example.

When we face dangers the amygdala releases hormones that trigger fear and limit our ability to use the compass of the heart.

In order to increase syntropy we need to become fearless and silence the chatter of the mind.

Many strategies can be used. What I found effective in my life (and was also effective for Steve Jobs) is Zen meditation. In this type of meditation participants don't react to their thoughts, they just observe them. Thoughts wait for the reaction of the heart. When the heart reacts it provides energy to the thought amplifying it, when it doesn't react the thought dissolves.

We are the heart. When the heart decides to be silent; the mind becomes silent. Our will is in the heart. When we discover that the scepter of command is in the heart without difficulty we can connect with the Attractor and fulfill the mission of our life.

Silencing the chatter of the mind and focusing on the heart can be found in many traditions. The groups of Friends (also known as Quakers) were started in 1650 by George Fox when he discovered that we can establish a direct contact with Deity. The practice is simple, people sit in a circle and are silent for about an hour. Shared silence helps to feel the heart.

Silencing the chatter of the mind and focusing on the heart is not a religion. It frees our being from the conditioning power of the words and leads to discover that when thoughts calm down we experience a new condition: to be without thinking. A state in which thoughts are produced only when required by the heart. A state in which the gap between a thought and the other is not empty, but it is pure and absolute potentiality. Being without thinking empowers the heart: our true will.

Another factor which influences the perception of the heart is what we eat.

John Hubert Brocklesby became a vegetarian in prison during the First World

War. For him, Christians did not have to kill other Christians and he decided to be a conscientious objector. He was arrested and imprisoned. He had to face court martial. He knew he would be sentenced to death and he was terrified at the idea.

Another conscientious objector told him: «*If you talk with your heart it is God who speaks through you.*» This gave him courage. Then this same conscientious objector added: «*If you do not eat meat, the voice of the heart becomes stronger.*» He became a vegetarian in prison to serve the will of God and face court martial. A book was written using his diaries.[40]

We have no claws to hunt, our teeth are suitable for fruit and we have a long digestive system not intended for meat. The attractor towards which our species is converging has vegetarian features. Therefore, being vegetarian helps the connection with the attractor and with the heart.

Many other diets seem to increase the

---

[40] Jones WE, *We Will Not Fight: The Untold Story of World War Ones Conscientious Objectors,*
www.amazon.com/dp/1845133005/

perception of the heart.

Rudolf Steiner[41] believed that matter is condensed light (he used the word light with the same meaning of syntropy). If matter is condensed syntropy, there must be many different ways to transform the invisible (syntropy) into the visible (matter). Our visible environment is immersed in an invisible environment that offers incredible possibilities. Steiner believed that life was impossible without syntropy (ie without light), since syntropy is the vital energy that we continuously and directly absorb. He believed that it is possible to live only on syntropy (water). According to Steiner, the act of digesting stimulates the body to absorb the vital energy from the invisible, which is transformed and condensed into substances that maintain and build our body. Steiner used the following example: when we eat a potato,

---

[41] Rudolf Steiner (1861-1925) was an Austrian philosopher, social reformer, architect and esotericist who founded the anthroposophy movement. He attempted to formulate a spiritual science, a synthesis between science and spirituality that applied the clarity of scientific thought, of Western philosophy, to the spiritual world.

we chew and digest and this leads to absorbing the vital forces from our etheric environment and condensing them into substances. In other words, our body acquires structure and substance absorbing syntropy.

Michael Werner, born in 1949 in northern Germany and CEO of a pharmaceutical research institute in Arlesheim, became liquidarian in January 2001 and since then drinks only water and does not eat solid food. In his book *Life from Light*[42] Werner says that:

> *"I found that my conversion to living without food went extraordinarily well. I expected to feel weaker and weaker during the first few days. But then I began to realize that in my case this weakness did not exist. Instead I experienced a growing feeling of lightness during the day and a decrease in the amount of sleep I needed during the night. Going through this process was probably the most intense experience of my adult life."*

---

[42] Werner M., *Life from Light*,
www.amazon.it/dp/1905570058

If it is true that one can live and be fit and healthy without eating, incredible scenarios open up about human life and life in general.

Werner notes that being liquidarian is different from fasting:

"It is something completely different! With fasting the body mobilizes reserves of energy and matter and one cannot fast for an unlimited time, nor can one be without drinking. But the process I was undertaking was and remains a mental-spiritual phenomenon that requires a particular inner predisposition. In reality there is a condition: opening up to the idea of being able to be nourished by the etheric, by prana or by whatever it may be called. This is the necessary requirement. Then it will happen. I live liquidarism as a gift from the spiritual world."

Michael Werner emphasizes that the only prerequisite for feeding on light (ie syntropy) is to trust it. He uses the words of Steiner:

"There is a fundamental essence of our earthly material existence from which all matter is produced through a process of condensation. What is the

fundamental substance of our terrestrial existence? Spiritual science gives this answer: every substance on earth is condensed light! There is nothing but condensed light ... Wherever you touch a substance, there you have condensed light. All matter is, in essence, light."

NEEDS

Water is the lymph that provides syntropy to life. Without water life is unable to counteract the destructive effects of entropy and dies. We can therefore list water among the vital needs.

Life also needs heat. This is why the Sun is so important. The chlorophyll process absorbs energy and heat from the Sun and without the Sun life could not exist on this planet.

Life dies when water freezes. Heat is needed to keep life away from low temperatures.

Living systems are generally not able to feed directly on syntropy. Therefore they must meet conditions for the acquisition of food. These conditions are known as material needs.

When these needs are not met, alarm bells are activated, such as thirst for the need for water, hunger for food and chill for the need for heat.

These alarm bells are well known to all. We know how to associate them with the need that must be met and we know what we must do.

But we also have invisible vital needs !!!

We establish the connection with the source of syntropy (the attractor) through the autonomic nervous system, the solar plexus (ie the heart).

Since syntropy concentrates energy, a good connection with the attractor is perceived as warmth and well-being in the solar plexus. On the contrary, a weak connection is signaled by feelings of emptiness and pain that we usually indicate as anxiety and by symptoms of the autonomic nervous system, such as nausea, dizziness and suffocation.

Syntropy is needed to regenerate damaged cells and parts of the organism. The autonomic nervous system acts like a mechanic who consults the manufacturer's guide to carry out repairs and keeping the system as close as possible to the design. However, the design is not mechanical and the instructions are written with a magical ink, the ink of love (syntropy).

The autonomic nervous system is in charge of all the involuntary functions of the body and is responsible for controlling the movement of muscles and limbs and regulates body functions that are not subject to decisions and that do not require the conscious mind. For example, it is responsible for digestion, heart rate, food assimilation and cells regeneration.

These processes are completely unknown to our conscious mind. We don't know how they are performed and often we don't even know they exist. We don't need to be a doctor or a biologist to digest food or regenerate tissues. The body knows everything and shows an extraordinary level of intelligence. It directs and regulates these processes, thus expressing the capacity and potentials of an intelligence that is incredibly superior to our conscious mind.

It develops patterns of behavior that it then performs autonomously and automatically and that are maintained over time, giving rise to habits that are then stored, at least in part, in the muscles of the body. Behavioral patterns are repeated until they are activated automatically, regardless of our will. These patterns are then firmly placed in the memory of the unconscious mind. The conscious mind often does not know what is in the memory of the unconscious mind. As a result, the unconscious mind can open incredible scenarios in the processes of knowing ourselves. The autonomic nervous system (ie the unconscious mind) also acts as a guardian of any information that the conscious mind cannot handle.

When the connection with the attractor is strong we feel warmth, well-being and love, when it is weak we feel void, pain and anxiety accompanied by loneliness and isolation. When the connection with the attractor is absent the autonomic nervous system is not able to provide syntropy to the vital functions and the organism dies.

We can therefore die not only because of unsatisfied material needs, but also because of the lack of connection with the attractor.

The need for connection with the attractor is usually perceived as a ***need for love*** and cohesion.

To respond to our needs, we build maps of

the physical environment that lead to realize that we live in a world that has expanded towards infinity. On the contrary, consciousness concentrates towards the infinitely small.

The identity conflict arises from the comparison:

$$\frac{I}{Outside\ World} = 0$$

When I compare myself to the outside world I am equal to zero

By comparing ourselves with the physical reality we realize that we are equal to zero and this contradicts the feeling we exist.

This conflict is well described in Shakespeare's Hamlet *"to be or not to be"*. Not being is incompatible with life. To continue to respond to the challenges of life we need to find a purpose, a meaning, otherwise it is all useless.

The identity conflict leads to a vital **need for meaning** which, when not satisfied, causes feelings of worthlessness and depression.

Depression is an unsustainable type of suffering and people face it trying to expand their Ego, limiting the size of the world they compare to or simply erasing the outside world.

But, however we manipulate the numerator and/or the denominator of the identity conflict equation the result continues to be always equal to zero.

The need for meaning is an invisible need. Most people are not aware of it, but still it is vital and we must constantly respond to it.

We must all give meaning to our life and to do so we often accept the most incredible contradictions.

The identity conflict equation suggests a solution.

$$\frac{I \times \cancel{Outside\ World}}{\cancel{Outside\ World}} = I$$

When I compare myself to the outside world
and I am united to it through love, I am equal to myself

This is called the *Theorem of Love* and shows that:

- only when our inner world unites with the outside world through love, we overcome the identity conflict;
- love provides this unity (I x Outside World), and therefore love is vital: it gives meaning to life;
- love allows to shift from duality (I = 0) to unity (I = I).

When we love, we converge towards unity and our heart fills with warmth, well-being and happiness. When we do not love, we diverge and we experience pain, emptiness and loneliness and our life is meaningless.

Let's recap:

- The first group of vital needs is commonly known as **material needs**. To combat the dissipative effects of entropy, living systems must acquire syntropy through water, energy and food, they must protect themselves from the dissipative effects of entropy and eliminate the remains of the destruction of structures by entropy. These conditions include shelter, clothing, waste disposal and hygiene. The partial satisfaction of material needs is signaled by hunger, thirst and various forms of suffering. Total dissatisfaction leads to death.

— The second vital need is commonly called the ***need for love***. Responding to material needs does not prevent entropy from destroying life. For example, cells die and must be replaced. To repair the damage caused by entropy, we must draw on the regenerative properties of syntropy which allow to create order, reconstruct structures and increase the levels of organization. The autonomic nervous system, which supports vital functions, acquires syntropy. Since syntropy acts as an absorber and energy concentrator, the intake of syntropy is felt in the thoracic area of the autonomic nervous system, in the form of warmth and well-being that we usually indicate as love;

the lack of syntropy is perceived as emptiness and pain in the thoracic area, usually referred to as anxiety. In short, the need to acquire syntropy is felt as a need for love. When this need is not satisfied there is suffering in the form of emptiness and pain. When this need is totally unsatisfied, living systems are not able to sustain the regenerative and vital processes and entropy takes over, bringing the system to death.

— The third vital need is commonly called the **need for meaning**. In order to satisfy material needs we produce maps of the environment. These maps give rise to the identity conflict. Entropy has inflated the physical universe towards infinity, while syntropy concentrates consciousness in extremely limited spaces. As a result, when we compare ourselves to the infinity of the universe, we discover that we are equal to zero. On the one hand we feel we exist, on the other we are aware of being equal to zero. These two opposing considerations *"to be or not to be"* cannot coexist. The identity conflict is characterized by lack of meaning, lack of energy, existential crisis and depression, generally perceived in the form of tensions in the head accompanied by anxiety. Being equal to zero is equivalent to death, which is incompatible with our feeling of existing. From this arises a vital need for meaning.

The solution to suffering is provided by the Theorem of Love. The Theorem of Love requires that we rely on the heart (the solar plexus) and use it consciously and intentionally to go towards the most beneficial options.

However, nowadays people mainly face their need for meaning trying to increase their Ego and this causes conflicts, difficulties in cooperation and greed. This is probably one of the biggest problems in the path towards the transformation that is required in order for humanity to win the challenges posed by the incoming ice-age.

The need for meaning arises from the identity conflict between being and not being:

$$\frac{I}{Outside\ World} = 0$$

and the *Theorem of Love* shows that the solution is provided by love.

However, people use strategies aimed to increase or decrease the numerator and/or denominator of the identity conflict equation, among which three strategies are commonly used.

n ° 1: Expand the Ego (ie increase the numerator)

To reduce depression, we try to expand our Ego through wealth, power, approval and popularity.

$$\frac{I + judgments + wealth + popularity + power + \cdots}{Outside\ World} = 0$$

When we expand our Ego depression vanishes for a few seconds. This brief relief leads to reiterate, to want to expand our Ego more and more.

For example, if we expand our Ego thanks to the approval of others, we will increasingly seek approval and to this end we will have to meet their expectations by behaving in ways that others judge positively. We will begin to use masks and others will see our masks and not our true self. This will make us feel lonely and without love and will increase the identity conflict and depression.

the more we need approval, the less we are spontaneous
the more we use masks, the more we feel alone
the identity conflict increases and we need more
approval

To be approved we must be part of a group. Without other people, it is impossible to receive positive judgments. Others are the source of our value and this generates social pressure and the fear of being rejected.

In a famous experiment, Stanley Milgram[43] showed how social pressure can be coercive. The purpose of Milgram's experiment was to study to what extent people were willing to obey orders which were clearly wrong.

Milgram used volunteers divided into pairs, the first volunteer was asked to play the role of the teacher, while the second volunteer was the student. The student was taken to a nearby room and seated on a kind of electric chair, then entrusted with the task of memorizing a list of words. The teacher was given the task of listening to the student and of sending electric shocks when he was wrong.

The teacher used a switch. At the first error he was asked to send a shock of 15 volts, then 30 volts for the second error, 45 volts for the third error and so on, with regular successions up to 450 volts. Every six increases in the intensity of the shock a voice warned: *weak shock, medium shock, strong shock, dangerous shock.*

---

[43]Milgram S. (1974), *Obedience to Authority: An Experimental View,* Harpercollins, New York, 1974.

Milgram explained to the teacher that the intensity of the shock had to be increased with each error. When the list was long and difficult, the answers were often wrong and the teacher was asked to send stronger and stronger shocks. At 75 volts the students started complaining, at 150 they asked to interrupt the experiment, but Milgram ordered to continue. At 180 volts, the students started screaming because they couldn't stand the pain anymore. If the teacher showed any hesitation, Milgram ordered to continue, even when the students, at 300 volts, shouted desperately to be freed.

The purpose of the experiment was to study to what extent the teacher was willing to follow orders. He did not know that the student was a collaborator of Milgram and that he received no electric shocks. The student was in another room, his prayers and screams were not real but they were recorded.

A group of psychiatrists estimated in advance that most teachers would stop at 150 volts, when the students started shouting for help. The results of the experiment, however, were surprisingly different: over 80% of the teachers continued the experiment even after 150 volts, and 62% of these continued up to 450 volts.

However, it was not easy for teachers to obey. Many began to sweat, but were ordered to continue to increase the intensity of the shocks. Disobedience was easier when Milgram was not present and when orders were given by telephone, from a nearby room. Many teachers claimed to execute orders, but the students received weaker shocks than they should have. On the other hand, teachers obeyed more easily if the victims were far away; 30% agreed to force students to hold hands on a metal plate that was supposed to transmit very strong shocks, but if the victim was in another room and the protest was limited to kicking the wall, the percentage of obedience exceeded 60%.

The experiment shows that teachers were unable to disobey to orders which were clearly wrong.

Without other people it is impossible to receive approval. Others are the source of our approval and this generates a deep need for consent and the fear of being rejected. To be accepted we need social inclusion. The fear of being isolated leads to obey the group, even going against the foundations of ethics.

Another way to expand our Ego is the equivalence "*I am what I have*". Examples are provided by money, popularity, wealth and power. Money, wealth, popularity and power make our Ego expand and cause greed. Whatever value we put to the numerator, if compared with the infinity of the universe, the result is always equal to zero. We can become emperors of the planet and continue to feel depressed. We can reach the highest levels of power, where we decide the life or death of people, but we still continue to feel equal to zero. The brief relief from depression turns these strategies into needs.

Many psychologists and sociologists have suggested specific needs for power, wealth and popularity[44]. The Theory of Vital Needs

---

[44] For example, the Need of Power (nPow) model developed by McClelland in 1975.

considers these secondary needs which develop from the vital need of meaning.

Everything we use to give meaning to our life becomes vital and consequently gains power.

Even ideologies, cultural systems and religions provide values and can therefore become vital. We defend our sources of value and this is one of the main causes of conflicts and an obstacle in our evolution towards happiness and well-being.

People live trapped in their values and when they are faced with diversity a shock can arise.

The unprepared visitor can experience a cultural shock when immersed in another culture. Immigrants often suffer from cultural shocks, depression and existential crises. Culture shocks happen to travelers who suddenly find in places where yes means no, where fixed prices are replaced by bargaining, where waiting is not an offense, where laughter can indicate anger and where the psychological signals familiar to us are replaced with new signals unknown to us and incomprehensible.[45]

---

[45]Toffler A, *Future Shock*, www.amazon.com/dp/0553277375

When a strategy provides a brief relief we repeat it. If we receive meaning through money we will want more money, if we receive it through beauty we want more beauty, if through power we will seek more power.

Power, wealth and popularity are based on the equivalence: *"I am because I have"*.

Erich Fromm in the book *"To Have or to Be?"* says:

"So if I am what I have, and what I have is lost, who am I? Nothing but a pathetic witness to a wrong lifestyle. Because I can lose what I have I live constantly in the fear of being deprived of what I own. I am afraid of thieves, of economic crises, I fear revolutions, diseases, death, love, freedom, changes and the unknown."[46]

---

[46] Fromm E., *To Have or to Be?* ww.amazon.com/dp/B00BBPWBAK

n ° 2: reduce the denominator

We can try to solve the identity conflict by decreasing the denominator, for example:

$$\frac{I}{Community} = 0$$

But only when we are totally part of the group does the equation become:

$$\frac{I \text{ x } \cancel{Community}}{\cancel{Community}} = I$$

and the conflict between being and non-being (I=0) disappears and we experience the identity (I=I).

This strategy is often used in combination with the first strategy which aims to expand the Ego.

The need for meaning is thus transformed into the need for belonging to a group. It becomes vital to be part of the group and be totally accepted by it. People do everything to ensure being accepted.

Many examples have been provided by history. One of the most surprising dates back to November 18, 1978, when 918 Americans decided to die in the Peoples Temple, led by Jim Jones.

This example shows that the scenario number 2, of a small elite which could survive the one hundred thousand years of glacial temperatures isolated from humanity and the world, will inevitably end in suicide.

The Peoples Temple had been founded in Indianapolis in the mid-1950s. After numerous criticisms of its integrationist ideas, the Temple moved to Redwood Valley, California, and in the early 1970s it opened other centers in San Fernando and San Francisco.

In the fall of 1973, after a series of articles and the defection of eight members from the Temple, Jones prepared an "immediate action" plan that listed various options, including the flight to Canada or a mission to the Caribbean, to Barbados or Trinidad. The Temple chose

Guyana and in 1974, after visiting northwestern Guyana, Jones negotiated a lease for over 15.4 km² of land, located 240 km west of the capital of Guyana, Georgetown.

Members began building Jonestown and Jones encouraged people to move to what was called the Peoples Temple agricultural project.

The relatively large number of Americans who arrived in Guyana tested the government's small but severe immigration infrastructure in a country where most people want to leave. Jones reached an agreement to ensure that Guyana would allow mass migration of Temple members, in exchange for investing most of the church's assets in Guyana. Immigration was asked to inhibit the departure of the deserters of the Temple and to reduce visas to opponents.

In the summer of 1976, Jones and several hundred members of the Temple moved to Jonestown to escape media investigations. After the mass migration, Jonestown had a population of just under a thousand people. Temple members attended study activities in a pavilion, including lectures on revolution and enemies. Entertainment activities were prohibited. Jones released long monologues about how his people had to "read" events. No TV and no films, no matter how harmless or seemingly politically neutral, were allowed. Jonestown's only means of communication with the outside world was a shortwave radio.

Although Jonestown did not have prisons, various forms of punishment were used against members considered unruly. The methods included torture and beatings, and this became the subject of rumors that spread among the locals in Guyana. Members who tried to escape were administered Thorazine, Pentathol, Demerol and Valium in "care units". Armed guards patrolled the area day and night to enforce the rules.

Children were delivered to the care of the community and turned to Jones as "Dad" and could only see their parents during the night. Jones was called "Father" or "Dad" even by adults.

Money that arrived every month as payment for pensions ended up in the Temple and the Temple's wealth was estimated at $ 26 million.

Jones often spoke of the risk that the CIA and other intelligence agencies were preparing plans to destroy Jonestown and eliminate its inhabitants. Mass suicide was regularly simulated:

"Everyone, including children, was told to queue up to get a glass of red drinking liquid. We were told that the liquid contained poison and that we would die within 45 minutes. We did everything we were told."

The Temple received half a kilo of cyanide per month for the jewelry workshop. In May 1978, a Temple doctor wrote to Jones asking for permission to test cyanide on Jonestown pigs, as their metabolism was similar to that of humans.

Jones was becoming increasingly paranoid and kept long monologues on the drastic escalation of repression.

According to Odell Rhodes, one of the escaped members of the Temple, the first to take the poison was Ruletta Paul and her one-year-old child. A syringe with the needle removed was used to spray the poison into the baby's mouth and then Ruletta took her dose. Mothers with their children approached the table and Jones encouraged them to take the poison. The poison caused death within five minutes. After ingesting the poison, people were escorted along a wooden walkway that led out of the pavilion.

Jones repeated:

"Die with dignity, do not die with tears and anguish ... death is a million times better than ten other days of this life. If only you knew what they are preparing, you'd be glad to die tonight."

Odell Rhodes stated that while the poison was being sprayed into the children's mouth, he did not observe panic, people seemed in a trance.

Jones was found dead lying in his chair between two other bodies, his head sprawled on a pillow.

The mass suicide of Jonestown shows how far people can come to be accepted by the community and thus respond to the need for meaning and how they can become temporarily blind, in a state of trance, and commit otherwise unthinkable acts.

The events of Jonestown constitute the largest loss of American civilians in a non-natural disaster until 11 September 2001.

n ° 3. Cancel the outside world

When increasing our value and reducing the outside world is no longer enough, another strategy is to erase the outside world.
The identity conflict formula turns into:

$$\frac{I \times I}{I} = I$$

This strategy explains 3 types of psychiatric disorders and underlines that the scenario 2 of an elite which will survive the ice age erasing the outside world will inevitably end into psychiatric disorders, such as:

- when (I x I) prevails, people can develop a narcissistic personality disorder.
- When (I / I) prevails we have a paranoid personality disorder.
- When (I / I) and (I x I) have similar weights, we have a psychotic disorder.

A common feature of these disorders is the closure in oneself and the perception of the external world as threatening or inappropriate in relation to one's expectations.

In the *narcissistic personality disorder* love for ourselves dominates (I x I). Individuals who develop a narcissistic personality disorder believe that they are special and unique. They expect to receive approval and praise for their superior qualities and often are proud and arrogant. By virtue of the personal values that they believe they possess, they want to be with prestigious people of high social or intellectual level. Finally, they are often taken from fantasies of unlimited success, power, beauty or ideal love. Because the outside world has been replaced by their Ego, these individuals show a lack of sensitivity to the needs and feelings of others. They lack empathy and can easily abuse others without regard to the consequences. Furthermore, others are idealized as long as they satisfy the need for admiration and gratification. Relationships tend to be emotionally cold and detached, regardless of the pain they generate in others. These people tend to break rather than strengthen bonds.

In the *paranoid personality disorder* the I/I fraction dominates and we replace the external world. But because we live in the identity conflict, we perceive the external world as threatening and find it difficult to distinguish the inner world of depression from the outside world. The sense of threat is considered to be objective, absolute and certain, not a subjective experience, a fantasy or a hypothesis. Sometimes our inner feelings are derision, and at other times they are derogatory or provocative and we begin to believe that we are unjustly victims of a hostile and humiliating world. We begin to experience anger, resentment and irritation and react aggressively. When, on the other hand, the impression is that of being excluded, feelings of anxiety and sadness prevail, accompanied by withdrawal from the world. Individuals with this disorder may also be insanely jealous and may suspect, without a real reason, that their spouse or partner is unfaithful. These individuals are unable to put themselves in the perspective of others and to distinguish their points of view from those of other people.

In *psychotic disorders* the I/I fraction and the IxI multiplication prevail. People replace the external reality with their inner world. They project their suffering and their fears outside themselves in the form of hallucinations and ideas of being unworthy, incapable and unfit. These considerations can take the form of delusions, an illogical thoughts supported by convictions and absurdities that are not accepted by others. The outside world is transformed into threatening and persecutory voices that are a constant reminder of the total lack of meaning of one's existence. The voices are often characterized by paranoid beliefs of a world that conspires against us, combined with hallucinations typical of schizophrenia and psychosis that lead to unbearable levels of suffering, so high as to push the person towards suicide, which is perceived as the only way out.

Since we have $I \times I$ in the numerator of the identity conflict equation, people who suffer from hallucinations are also characterized by extreme social withdrawal and isolate themselves in their imaginary world. Social withdrawal, in turn, leads to becoming more introverted and these people only worry about their symptoms and illness. This results in additional traits, typical of psychosis and schizophrenia, such as selfishness, insensitivity and lack of interest in the feelings of others.

THE NEW MONETARY SYSTEM

One of the first steps towards creating the conditions which will allow humanity to face the challenges of the ice age is to shift from the nowadays entropic monetary system to a new monetary system which amplifies the properties of syntropy (energy concentration and absorption).

Similarly to a lymph which responds to visible and invisible vital needs a new monetary system will promote syntropy, life and wellbeing.

The entropic monetary system based on private central banks preys on nature, people and nations looting their vital energies and causing crises, wars, destruction, suffering, illnesses and debts.

On the contrary, the "syntropic monetary system" nourishes life, people, nations with vital energy, generating wealth, wellbeing and happiness.

The syntropic monetary system:

— acknowledges that value originates from the needs of people and therefore provides an unconditional basic income to each citizen.

— Money authority is not private but public. Private central banks are replaced by the Treasury and the Social Security.

— When there is inflation the unconditional basic income is reduced and/or taxes are increased, when there is deflation the unconditional basic income is increased and/or taxes reduced.

— The State cannot borrow money, but only receive it through taxes. There is no indebtment of the State.

— Since there is no debt to pay back and no interests on the debt, taxes are low.

— Loans can only be part of a partnerships where lender and client share profits and risks. Interests are illegal.

— Entropy reduction is a priority which leads to optimize and increase the quality of life. Whatever increases entropy and is damaging for life is discouraged or banished. This leads to limit taxation to a flat tax which never exceeds 10% and which is applied to all the money transactions, making tax returns no longer necessary.

— Anonymous non traceable money is illegal since it favors entropic activities. Paper money, Bit Coins or other privately owned systems of money are illegal and replaced by bioelectronic (traceable) money under the authority of the Treasury. Bioelectronic money reduces entropy and increases syntropy, restoring confidence among citizens and the State.

— Bioelectronic money requires bioelectronic identification. Citizens who are not registered have no access to money. Invisible residents and illegal migrants have no access to money.

— The syntropic monetary system requires the transition from representative democracy to direct democracy and meritocracy.

— The syntropic monetary system focuses on the accomplishment of the *Theorem of Love*.

Let us see some examples.

- Bioelectronic identification

On September 29, 2010, India founded the UIDAI (Unique Identification Authority of India), an agency of the Government of India which is responsible for the centralized database which provides bioelectronic identification of the population.

Biometric parameters allow instant and reliable identification of people.

Each Indian citizen receives an identification number of 12 characters, associated with biometric information (photograph, fingerprint and iris), demographic information and an electronic deposit account. This system does not include information that may lead to discrimination such as caste, religion and political beliefs.

UIDAI was inaugurated by Prime Minister Manmohan Singh and the initial goal was to develop a system which permits to distribute aid directly to the people without intermediaries, providing money in the electronic deposit accounts, and solving the problems encountered during elections, where a few people were able to manipulate results by playing on the uncertainty of identity.

In the West we usually associate identification with the reduction of freedom, but according to the Indian project just the opposite happens. A person with no identity is, in fact, a person deprived of rights. He/she cannot vote, receive welfare benefits, work regularly and be protected by the law. Identification opens the door to rights and security and allows citizens to become part of a modern economy.

Indians collaborated with great enthusiasm in the UIDAI system and in the aftermath of the 2016 withdrawal of 87% of paper money, bioelectronic digital payments have become an instant hit.

A key condition is the fact that the RBI (the Reserve Bank of India, India's Central Bank), which originally started as a private entity, was nationalized in 1949, when India became independent from the British Empire. RBI's directors have since then been appointed by the government and RBI is owned by the government of India, as it is clearly stated in the Reserve Bank of India Act.

On the one hand, bioelectronic identification provides citizen with rights, on the other the government receives information useful to plan policies such as those relating to food, water and energy distribution, construction of infrastructures, housing, urban mobility, hospitals and schools.

India is a country where a large size of the population still lives in poverty and which is not yet able to address some of the basic needs of the population. However, bioelectronic identification favors cooperation, wealth, health, education and welfare policies.

Paper money is anonymous and allows to avoid taxes and engage in corruption. For example, in India real estate sales were often split into two parts: a smaller portion, which was reported to the government, paid by check, and a larger, undeclared sum paid with stacks of paper money, or "black money." Businessmen and criminals used to buy government officials and politicians with envelopes and briefcases filled with paper money.

The end of paper money and anonymous financial transactions has the power to reduce illegality and restore confidence among citizens and institutions. It makes it impossible for a public official to ask for money in order to "speed up" paperwork. It is no longer possible to steal money and act against the common good.

Without paper money illegal migration becomes impossible. Each individual wants bioelectronic identification in order to have money.

- No debts no interests

The Southeast Asian *Guānxi* system provides an interesting example. Guānxi means network of intimate relationships.

Chinese children learn to share food, toys and money in the belief that: "*one finger alone can do nothing, but in one hand it acquires power.*"

By sharing they learn to build relationships of trust, honesty, fairness and reciprocity which then become their guānxi (close relations networks).

Guānxis are the pillar of the Chinese society and of the Southeast Asian societies. They differentiate the East from the West, and make China so incomprehensible to Westerners.

Any Chinese gives total dedication to his guānxi and knows that when needed he will receive any help from it. Guānxis are the basic asset of any person living in Southeast Asia.

This system of sharing and cooperation has its roots in the rice farming tradition:

"a history of farming rice makes people more interdependent, whereas farming wheat makes individuals more independent, and these agricultural legacies continue to affect people in the modern world."[47]

---

[47] Talhelm T, Zhang X, Oishi S, Shimin C, Duan D, Lan X and Kitayama S (2014), *Large-Scale Psychological Differences Within China Explained by Rice Versus Wheat Agriculture*, Science, 9 May 2014: vol. 344, no. 6184, pp. 603-608, DOI:10.1126/science.1246850.

Rice farming is extremely labor-intensive, requiring about twice the number of hours from planting to harvest as does wheat. Because most rice is grown on irrigated land, it requires the sharing of water and the building of dikes and canals that constantly need maintenance. Rice farmers must work together to develop and maintain an infrastructure upon which all depend and this leads to a cooperative and collective mindset. Wheat, on the other hand, is grown on dry land, it relies on rain for moisture. Farmers are able to depend more on themselves and this leads to a more individualistic mindset.

During holidays, anniversaries and birthdays Chinese give red envelopes containing money. Since the spring of 2015 red envelopes have also become electronic, and in the first 24 hours of 2016 WeChat, the Chinese messaging system, has seen sending 2.3 billion electronic red envelopes.

In marriages red envelopes reach their peak. Invitees deliver the offer for the newlyweds in a red envelope. A cashier at the entrance of the restaurant opens the envelope and writes in a public register the name and surname of the guest and the amount. Chinese spouses receive on average (in Europe) between 250 thousand and 400 thousand euros. Enough to buy a house or start a business.

Red envelopes are an example of the traditional Chinese culture of sharing and cooperation that originates from rice.

The average Chinese puts aside at least one third of his/her income. The money saved, however, does not end in the bank, but is given to those in the guānxi, who want to start a new activity. When a Chinese ventures into the world his guānxi provides support and money. The guānxi is the social capital, the wealth on which every Chinese relies.

Guānxis are built on trust and reciprocity. Who receives without giving is a 黑人 *hei rén*, a corrupt person, decadent and reactionary, contrary to the principle of sharing. For Chinese *hei rén* is the ultimate infamy and leads to exclusion, "*a finger alone that can do nothing.*"

To be accepted in a guānxi, the person must feel you in his heart. As long as this heart feeling is missing, people are not allowed into the guānxi and relations are only formal. Guānxis are networks of trust, based on the certainty that people will not betray you.

Paper contracts imply the absence of trust and they are considered a sign of decadence. In the West trust has failed, the social fabric has disintegrated and transactions are based on written contracts, that are often not honored. Guānxi requires trust and the focus on the heart, which in China is considered to be the core. Chinese have difficulties understanding Westerners who behave like *hei rén*, corrupt people, decadent and reactionary. Mixing East and West is complex. Our corrupt culture can easily fascinate young people, whereas it is more difficult to evolve towards the values of cooperation and sharing typical of Southeastern Asia.

Guānxis cannot be improvised. They are built with patience throughout life and last a lifetime. It is an extended family that involves a series of mutual aid modalities through which Chinese build together their future.

It is a principle of reciprocity which is manifested in the long term and usually takes place at the right time, maybe with demonstrations of generosity, in a kind of "escalation of gratitude."

The ability to build a guānxi ensures the success and future of both individuals and organizations. For this reason for Chinese people it is more important to give than to receive. The guānxi system allows to grow, it is a safety net, but also an obligation always present:

"I am an entrepreneur, I have twenty employees, but when a worker wishes to start his own activity I am obliged to give my contribution. (...) Two months ago one of my workers bought an appliance store. He received from me 12,000 Euros."

While in the West the savings rate is around zero, or in some countries even negative, because people spend more than they earn, borrowing money from the banks, the average Chinese sets aside half of his/her income. The money which is saved, however, is not put in a bank, but invested in the guānxi. This, after some years will allow to ask maybe 100,000 euros or more to open a restaurant or start a business.

Chinese wealth and businesses are based on the guānxi culture. This makes them profoundly difficult to understand for Westerners. The difficulties that Western entrepreneurs face in China is mainly linked to the guānxi culture.

It is in difficult moments that guānxis give their best.

For example, during the SARS[48] many owners of restaurants found themselves with no customers and with very big financial problems. If they had been exposed with banks they would have lost the restaurants. The guānxi system solved the crisis, but it also has requirements. The important thing is that the entrepreneur demonstrates to their guānxi that he is putting his heart into his activity. It is clear that such a system can only work if all the individuals are going in the same direction, if there is total trust, and common aims are

---

[48] Severe Acute Respiratory Syndrome (SARS) a form of atypical pneumonia which appeared for the first time in November 2002 in the Guangdong province of China

shared. Success is based on the utmost confidence in each other.

But, working with the Western world challenges the guānxi system. Chinese manufacturers usually send goods, even a whole container, without requiring advanced payments or signed contracts. In recent years, however, a growing number of Chinese have found themselves in difficulties because of the unreliability of Western clients who often do not pay or pay late.

Due to the unreliability of the Western clients several Chinese failed to pay for goods from China, thus contravening the principle of trust which is at the basis of the guānxi and forcing Chinese suppliers to start demanding payments in advance, especially for goods sent to countries where it has become a practice not to pay. Consequently Chinese manufacturers now require a deposit of at least half the value of the goods when sending containers to Europe.

In the guānxi system interests and debts are banned. The person who has received money from its guānxi does not have a debt and is not expected to pay interests. Though, when other people in the guānxi need, he/she will contribute freely according to his possibilities.

The guānxi system of giving and receiving is at the basis of the incredible ability of Chinese people to produce wealth.

It is a win-win financial system, since the risk and benefits are shared. The western system, instead, is a "risk transfer" system, where the creditor always wins even when the debtor loses.

- Paper money and criminality

The end of paper money and anonymous financial transactions has the power to reduce illegality and restore confidence among citizens.

With bioelectronic money, sellers don't have to give change because the exact amount of money is always paid and it is always possible to check how much was paid. Bribes and corruption become impossible since bioelectronic money always leaves a trace and it is never anonymous. Suppliers can check if the client has been paid and in turn require the payment for their work. Robbery and common crime become impossible. Citizens can control the spending of public money, thus preventing administrative frauds.

A description of the devilish nature of paper money was clearly provided by Gary Webb in the book "Dark Alliance", published in 1999.

Investigating the sharp increase in cocaine and crack addicts in the slums of American big towns, Webb discovered that drug dealers were protected by the CIA, with the complicity of the DEA, DIA and FBI. Local authorities were forbidden to arrest drug dealers and the CIA protected international smugglers, allowing the entry of large quantities of cocaine into the United States. In return, the CIA demanded a share of revenues in paper money (anonymous money) which was then used to finance activities prohibited by law and by the U.S. Congress.

In our win-lose system illnesses, wars, conflicts, tensions and natural disasters increase debts and provide power to the owners of the private central banks. This is the reason behind the limitless amount of money that is allocated for wars, whereas there is always no or little money for welfare and the promotion of wellbeing.

Gary Webb describes that the money made from drugs were used to support the illegal war in Nicaragua. Paper money played a key role. It made crack and cocaine readily available in the slums, destroying the lives of millions of Americans who became addicted, went to prison, died or became disabled and allowed to circumvent the prohibitions of the U.S. Congress.

In 2004, Webb was found dead with two bullets in his head. His work had caused great controversy, but eventually the governmental investigation initiated within the CIA, conducted by Inspector General Frederick Hitz, recognized the validity of the Webb report and discovered that the situation was even more severe than that which Webb himself had reported.

In order to counter the ice age one of the requirements is to shift from national currencies to a world bioelectronic currency under the control of a united identification system.

Syntropy increases cohesion and unity and at the same time it increase diversity and identity. The transition towards syntropy is a process which increases *"unity and diversity while converging"*. Consequently a syntropic monetary system should be named *"Unity in Diversity Converging"*. This idea is not new and was put forward by several authors, among which the *United Future World Currency* program that minted a limited number of the *Unity in Diversity* coins.

THE THIRD SCENARIO

At the age of 16 I won a scholarship to attend my last year of high school in the United States. I was hosted by an American family in Jefferson City, Missouri, a city of thirty thousand inhabitants in the heart of the United States. If you draw two diagonals that connect the ends of the United States, in the center there is Jefferson City. It was a place of bigotry and religious fanaticism, of phobia and terror of Russia and the communists and of a total absence of freedom of thought. If someone expressed a different idea, he was immediately accused of communist sympathies. Being a communist or having communist sympathies meant losing all rights and being marginalized. People were terrified of being suspected of communism and to avoid this they all conformed to the will of the *system*. There was no naturalness and there was great dissatisfaction. Young people made great use of drugs and alcohol. There were no spontaneous meeting places, such as the European "piazzas". People did not walk in the streets and the only way to meet and look for friends was to attend school or church clubs. Young people lived a deep solitude and felt alone in the midst of others. Even when in groups a profound solitude was felt. Love was regulated and not spontaneous. This situation was a real surprise for me. I found a country profoundly different from what I had imagined and seen in Hollywood movies. My year abroad soon became a nightmare. I experienced strong feelings of depression, anxiety and loneliness.

On April 2 (1976) I went to Joplin to meet other foreign students. After lunch I spent the entire afternoon talking to an Iranian boy, Sinai. We sat on the banks of a small artificial lake. I needed to understand what anxiety and depression were. Everyone around me seemed happy and I wondered if I was the only who suffered. Sinai told me that according to Islamic scientific thought there is another level besides matter and energy. He told me that physical energy diverges, while this other level is made of converging energy that leads to unity, love and cohesion. We started talking about this level and our imagination began to fly. A cohesive energy that, when it is felt, causes warmth and well-being in the solar plexus, similar to love. When it is not felt, emptiness, pain and anxiety are sensed. We came to imagine a future full of this energy, made of love and cohesion. A very different future from what I was experiencing in the United States. Suddenly I began to feel that life made sense and that the future of humanity was not war and destruction, but love.

Unexpectedly, depression and anxiety vanished.

That night I woke up at around 3.30. I was immersed in a luminescent orange haze that radiated warmth and love. In front of me there was a light so dense that it could be touched. A light that radiated love, well-being, peace and tranquility. I approached this light and suddenly saw the future of humanity flowing in front of me. A future full of life, well-being and love. A vision that took place in the twilight. I saw large transparent and luminescent structures, in which life flourished intensely. Then suddenly I was sucked into this dense orange light. I don't know how long it lasted. But when I came out of it, I felt an incredible feeling of love. I felt I had received a message, a message of fundamental importance that my rational mind could not understand. The light faded quickly. I tried to regain contact, but it dissolved, letting myself sink into the darkness of the room, into the cold and solitude. I felt a shiver down my back. I woke the person next to me and asked if he had seen or heard anything, but he told me to stop making noises, he wanted to keep sleeping. I tried to reconnect with this light of love, but I didn't know how.

That day in Joplin paved the way to the discovery of syntropy and the scenario of a humanity filled with love, that survives the challenges of time and evolves into a new era of wellbeing and happiness.

What I now know is that in order to survive the ice age we need to increase syntropy. Syntropy concentrates energy and increases temperatures, whereas entropy dissipates energy and decreases temperatures (thermal death).

The ice age provides a unique opportunity to shift from entropy to syntropy and accomplish a great leap forward towards love and the theorem of love.

It is now over 50 years that we have started entering the ice age, but the effects have not been felt yet thanks to the high levels of CO_2. CO_2 provide a warm blanket to the planet, preventing heat from dispersing and protecting the planet from cooling. But, according to Zharkova, we will witness the collapse of the Sun heat emissions in the early months of 2030 and then suddenly discover that we are in the ice age.

Life extinguishes during ice ages and this is the fate which expects us if we do not shift from entropy to syntropy. In 2030 countries like Britain might experience temperatures close to 100 degrees Celsius below zero. The Gulf Stream will stop and within a few centuries the entire planet, with the exception of the equatorial strip, will be covered with thick ice and become inhabitable.

The third scenario shows that the way out is based on the simple fact that while entropy leads to cooling, syntropy leads to warming. For millennia, humanity has chosen the way of entropy plundering the planet of its vital resources. Now we have to shift to the way of syntropy, promoting life and replenishing the vital resources of the planet.

The UDC is one of the first steps towards the new syntropic era, but it is not enough.

Life is the highest expression of syntropy and in order to increase syntropy we must maximize life.

Life absorbs energy and produces CO_2. The absence of life disperses energy and reduces CO_2.

In the syntropization of the planet one important step is afforestation and the reforestation of deserts and dry areas.

In China billions of trees are planted every year and deserts and dry lands are being transformed into forests. This process is helped by the fact that with the reduction of the Sun's emissions cosmic rays ionize the atmosphere and favor the formation of rain.

Agriculture is among the main causes of desertification. Syntropic agriculture[49] discovered by Ernst Götsch[50] blends forests with agriculture and shows that it is possible to turn deserts into forests within a few years.

Life produces CO_2: our breath, our activities produce CO_2 and CO_2 has the power to keep the planet from cooling. It is an invisible blanket that wraps the planet, reducing heat from dispersing into the void.

In order to increase CO_2 levels we must increase life and the population size. The problem is not overpopulation, but under-population.

The whole planet must become habitable, deserts must be turned into agroforests and our habits must change towards syntropy.

For example syntropic diet can reduce entropy by more than 500 times. Becoming vegetarian or vegan, is highly syntropic, increasing the energy balance and health. But

---

[49] https://lifeinsyntropy.org/en/
[50] https://www.agendagotsch.com/

also giving more attention to water and less to solid food can have incredible syntropic effects.

This is well described in the book *"Your Body's many Cries for Water"* written by the Iranian doctor Fereydoon Batmanghelidj.

Batmanghelidj completed his medical studies at St. Mary's Hospital in London and opened several clinics when he returned to Iran. However, during the 1979 Iranian revolution he was arrested and spent almost three years in prison in Tehran. A prison that was designed for 600 people, but which housed more than 9 thousand people.

Here is how Batmanghelidj describes his discovery:

"The nightmare of life and death in that hell hole threatened everyone and tested the courage and strength of the weak and the strong. It was then that the human body revealed to me some of its greatest secrets, secrets never understood by medical science. (...) One night, after about two months of imprisonment, that secret was revealed. It was about 11 pm. I woke up, one of my cell mates suffered from terrible stomach pains. He couldn't

walk alone. Others were helping him stand up. He suffered from peptic ulcer and needed medical attention. He was very ill, but I was not allowed to take any medicine with me. At this point the surprising event occurred! I gave him two glasses of water and the pain disappeared within minutes and he could stand on his own again."[51]

Due to extreme conditions in Tehran prison, Batmanghelidj was able to discover that many diseases can be healed simply with water. Batmanghelidj came to the conclusion that the lack of water is expressed not only by thirst and dry mouth, but also by a series of localized symptoms that serve to inform us about a local need for water. These local signs of dehydration take the form of pain and are usually interpreted as symptoms of illness and not the need for water. Batmanghelidj realized that we often mistake pains caused by a local dehydration situation for diseases.

Conventional medicine concentrates on the solid 25% and does not consider the role of

---

[51] Batmanghelidj F (1992), *Your Body's many Cries for Water,* www.watercure.com

water (the other 75% of the body), since it assumes that the solid part is the active principle and that all the functions of the body depend on the solid while water works only as a solvent that fills the space.

The human body is considered as a large "test tube" filled with different types of solids and water as a chemically inert and insignificant packaging material.

Conventional medicine assumes that solutes (substances dissolved or transported in the blood) regulate all the activities of the body, while it is assumed that the intake of water (the solvent) is generally well respected, since water is easily available.

Based on this hypothesis, medical research has been addressed to the study of solids that are considered responsible for the onset of diseases. To date, a dry mouth is the only recognized symptom of dehydration. However, according to Batmanghelidj, a dry mouth is only the ultimate symptom of extreme dehydration.

Dr. Batmanghelidj explains several diseases as a result of water deficiency: rheumatoid arthritis, hypertension, high cholesterol, excess body weight, asthma and some allergies.

Batmanghelidj says that the fundamental error of conventional medicine is to confuse dehydration with disease. This error inhibits the necessary preventive measures and the patient is not provided with sufficient water treatments to cure his suffering. At the first appearance of pain, the body should receive water. In contrast, conventional medicine provides drugs that block the symptoms of the lack of water and the consequent conversion of symptoms into chronic diseases and chronic dehydration.

Batmanghelidj suggests changing the medical paradigm, moving from a vision centered on the properties of the solute (solid matter ie past causes) to a vision centered on the properties of the solvent (water and syntropy).

Batmanghelidj states that the solvent (water) regulates the functions of the body, including the activities of all solutes (solids) dissolved in it.

In this new paradigm diseases are interpreted as disorders of the body's water metabolism (solvent metabolism).

Water carries nutrients, hormones and chemical messages and performs multiple vital functions. The balance between chemical and solid substances is restored by restoring the correct water balance. In light of these considerations, water becomes the natural cure for a wide spectrum of disorders and complications that are currently labeled as "diseases".

Changing our nutrition habits and focusing more on water the land and energy consumption per person can diminish by hundreds of times. Combining this with syntropic agroforestry it is possible to feed a world population of over one hundred billion people.

The ice-age requires that we change our habits choosing low-entropy and high-syntropic options. We can start this in any moment.

We live in a planet rich in CO_2, oil, gas and coal. We have huge reserves of CO_2 that will serve in critical moments. Solar emissions are not constant, and during the peak of the ice age we will need to increase the levels of CO_2, drawing on these vast natural reserves. It is therefore wise to preserve these reserves, switching to alternative energy sources. Even though solar emissions will decrease it will be useful to promote the production of alternative energies.

Finally, our cities were built after the Second World War using cement and are now starting to crumble. Cement has a short life expectancy and towns will need to be rebuilt choosing solutions that maximize syntropy and are suitable for the incoming ice age.

The best architectural designs for the ice age conditions are based on pyramidal structures, built with low entropy materials, capable of withstanding extreme stresses such as strong earthquakes.

Not having a roof, pyramids don't have to support the weight of snow and ice. Large-scale pyramids, which host self-sufficient communities, with their own energy and heat sources, will introduce into the atmosphere large amounts of CO_2 and help counter the low temperatures of the ice age.

A small example of a pyramid in extreme cold climates has been built in the early nineties by the CNR, the Italian National Research Centre, at 5050 meters of altitude, in the Khumbu Valley, in the Sagarmatha National Park, at the foot of the Everest on the Nepalese side.

The CNR build a glass pyramid named Pyramid Ev-K2-CNR.

www.evk2cnr.org

It is a pyramid of negligible size compared to those that will be needed during the ice age. However, it is located in a glacial environment and shows that the pyramidal shape allows to combine stability and resistance to atmospheric agents and earthquakes and the glass coating ensures the greenhouse effect that facilitates the concentration of solar thermal energy despite the glacial temperatures of the surrounding place. It is a totally self-sufficient structure.

The Ev-K2-CNR pyramid is a laboratory and observatory located at 5050 meters above the sea level, on the Nepalese side of Mount Everest. It is universally appreciated for the studies it allows to do at high altitudes. Ev-K2-CNR uses a methodology that favors sustainable development in extreme climatic and environmental conditions. Studies that require extreme conditions can be conducted at the pyramid which has become the object of interest of numerous national and international scientific institution, over 200 scientific institutions, universities, organizations and research institutions. Thousands of scientific missions and more than 400 researchers from all over the world carry out their scientific researches every year at the CNR pyramid.

It might be just fake news, but in 2012 a leading oceanographer, Dr Meyer Verlag, claimed to have found not one but two gigantic pyramids, three times the size of the Great Pyramid of Giza, on the ocean floor in the heart of the Bermuda Triangle.

Dr Meyer found the pyramids during a routine oceanographic survey in mid-April 2012 and he reported the discovery on the 29th of April, after he finished checking and rechecking the data.

His report to the scientific community and to newsmen in Freeport, Bahamas, included maps and sonar readings.

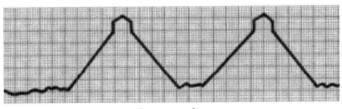

Sonar reading

Dr Verlag stated that the pyramids appeared

to be made of solid glass and were in such good conditions that he was almost certain that they were built within the past 50 years:

"Sonar readings taken from the surface indicate that the two pyramids are uncommonly large and in perfect condition. That would seem to indicate that the pyramids were built within the last 50 years or so and leads to more pressing questions such as who made them and why."

At the press conference held in the Bahamas he gave the exact coordinates of the pyramids, 800 miles east of Miami:

"Sonar data indicated that the bases of the pyramids are 2,000 feet (600 meters) wide. They stand almost 700 feet high and are roughly double the size of Egypt's Great Pyramid of Cheops. A superior technology is needed to build these pyramids. Whoever or whatever built them clearly had underwater capabilities far superior to our own. And while there's always room for error, our sonar readings suggest that the pyramids have the texture and density of glass which is most unusual indeed."

It seems that Pyramids are scattered across the planet, from America to Asia, archaeologists have found that nearly all ancient cultures built massive pyramids thousands of years ago. Some of them served as tombs, while the purpose of many other remains a mystery.

It isn't therefore surprising to learn that pyramids have been found also in Europe. The *Bosnian Pyramid Complex* was built by an unknown civilization near Sarajevo, the capital of Bosnia and Herzegovina.

These pyramids were discovered in 2015, by Dr. Semir Osmanagic, beneath the hills of Visoko. A pyramidal complex which in addition to being one of the largest on Earth, was interconnected through a network of underground tunnels.

Dr. Osmanagic claims that these pyramids provide the traces of a lost civilization.

His thesis holds that the Mesoamerican, the Egyptian and the Bosnian pyramids are the work of the same people and that the pyramidal complex in Bosnia could be "*the mother of all the pyramids."*

In 2006, a great project was set up to restore the top of the Pyramid of the Sun, which Dr. Osmanagic assures is the most important of the four Pyramids measuring 360 meters in height. The Bosnian Government made available the necessary funds for the excavation work in the Visoko region.

The decision of the Bosnian Government to fund the project raised a controversy in the European Association of Archaeologists, which in 2006 wrote the following letter against the decision of the Government of Bosnia and Herzegovina:

"We, the undersigned professional archaeologists from all parts of Europe, wish to protest strongly at the continuing support by the Bosnian authorities for the so-called "pyramid" project being conducted on hills at and near Visoko. This scheme is a cruel hoax on an unsuspecting public and has no place in the world of genuine science. It is a waste of scarce resources that would be much better used in protecting the genuine archaeological heritage and is diverting attention from the pressing problems that are affecting professional archaeologists in Bosnia-Herzegovina on a daily basis."

The letter was signed by Hermann Parzinger, President of the German Archaeological Institute in Berlin, Willem Willems, Inspector General of Rijksinspectie Archeologie in The Hague, Jean-Paul Demoule, President of the Institut nationale de recherches archéologiques préventives (INRAP) in Paris, Romuald Schild, Director of the Institute of Archaeology and Ethnology of the Polish Academy of Sciences in Warsaw, Vassil Nikolov, Director of the Institute of Archaeology of the Bulgarian Academy of Sciences in Sofia, Anthony Harding, President of the European Association of Archaeologists and Mike Heyworth, Director of the Council for British Archaeology in York.

But why did they go to this extent to stop the excavations? Some experts consider that this letter documents a massive cover-up.

A quality of pyramids made of transparent absorbing materials, in extreme environments such as those of the ice age, is that they will maximize the absorption of energy and heat. Not having a roof, snow or ice do not accumulate. Their broad base makes them stable and durable. When solar emissions diminish, the magnetic shield that protects the planet weakens and cosmic rays increase and activate the magma and earthquakes of strong intensity. Transparent pyramids can be self-sufficient from an energetic point of view and for food. They need air from outside and releases CO_2 and heat. Exactly what is needed during the ice age.

Depending on the conditions of the land the height could even reach a thousand meters with a square base of two kilometers per side. These pyramids can shelter special environments from the weight and destructive effect of ice. For example, a city like Rome, would be reduced to dust by the weight of the ice and its slow motion. Old historical places could be incorporated into the ground floor of the pyramids.

Pyramids of these proportions could be divided into levels up to 50 meters high. Independent levels with buildings, open spaces, gardens and public places such as piazzas, recreational and commercial areas, surrounded by nature and without mechanical noises and pollution, with trees, green area, birds, fishes and pets that can keep people in contact with nature. Unlike cities built using skyscrapers, where there are frequent deficiencies due to low exposure to the Sun, the shadow of the pyramids does not cover the other pyramids. Inhabitants of the pyramids will receive a fair exposure to the Sun, with considerable benefits for their health.

Structures of this kind could accommodate a hundred thousand people each. The excess heat, produced by the absorption of the Sun's rays and by the activities inside the pyramid, would be used to melt the snow, thus providing drinking water for life and its activities. According to some simulations, one million pyramids could compensate the effects of the ice age. They would occupy a total of three million square kilometers, one-fiftieth of the land of the planet. Some pyramids could be used only for productive activities or activities aimed at regulating the CO_2 levels of the planet.

They would be built using "soft matter" which is a material capable of withstanding the entire ice age and the most adverse conditions. A lightweight material that can repair itself and which has a positive energy balance. It is made of DNA which is highly resistant, flexible and can maintain the structure intact, autonomously, activating self-healing processes. Instead of following the law of entropy, that is thermal death and disorder, soft matter responds to the law of syntropy, concentrating and absorbing energy and heat. Just what is needed during the ice-age.

This "third scenario" focuses on syntropic agriculture, reforestation, pyramids, syntropic diet and habits and population increase.

With a world population that can produce enough CO_2 and heat to guarantee outside temperatures similar to those that we have today, people could continue to enjoy outdoor life, as we do today, going skiing, swimming, hiking.

Syntropic agriculture, pyramids, reforestation, population growth and changing our habits can win the ice age and can be achieved relatively quickly.

It is a unique undertaking, a challenge that humanity can win for the first time in the history of this planet. A challenge that will promote a leap forward in civilization and technology.

Key points of this scenario are: an intense reforestation of trillions of trees a year; the transition to renewable energies, the transition to syntropic agriculture; the promotion of policies of population increase; new housing structures and syntropic habits.

A detailed description of this scenario is available in "The Trilogy": www.sintropia.it .

Also the psychological side needs to be addressed adequately.

What could be the effect of being confined in artificial structures like the pyramids for long periods of time? What will be the meaning of life of people living in these structures. How can we prevent inner emptiness and existential crises from exploding? Psychological and emotional distress could lead the entire project to collapse from within, and not from the outside. Attention must be given to these existential aspects and the solution is provided by the *Theorem of Love.*

A society that lives in love will not be able to suffer from depression and existential crises. The focus must be on the Theorem of Love.

The Theorem of Love requires that we shift from duality to non-duality, harmonizing the entropic and syntropic sides. This harmonization, this union of entropy and syntropy is possible only through love and the ice-age will help us in this process.

Ultimately the ice-age could lead humanity to Teilhard's Omega Point, solving the identity conflict between being and not being and the existential crisis.

FROM DUALITY TO UNITY

The first law of thermodynamics states that energy is a unity that cannot be created or destroyed, but only transformed. Entropy and syntropy are the two sides of this unity, linked together in a dynamic process of energy transformation. Entropy and syntropy cannot exist without each other. This dynamic interaction pervades all aspects of the universe and that is why everything vibrates and everything is dual.

In 1665, the Dutch mathematician and physicist Christian Huygens, among the first to postulate the wave theory of light, observed that, putting side by side two pendulums, these tended to tune their oscillation as if "*they wanted to take the same rhythm.*" Huygens discovered the phenomenon we now call resonance. In the case of two pendulums, it is said that one makes the other resonate at its own frequency.

All the manifestations of the universe are a continuous vibration between polarities: the yin and the yang, the converging and divergent forces, syntropy and entropy, absorbers and emitters.

In life, this takes the form of waves, pulsations and rhythms: the pulsations of the heart, the phases of the breath, light and sound waves.

All aspects of reality vibrate and these vibrations create resonances. An example is provided by tuning forks that vibrate at a frequency of 440 Hz. When a vibrating tuning fork is placed near a *"silent"* tuning fork, this second tuning fork begins to vibrate. Tuning forks vibrate only when exposed to a sound with their own resonance.

Resonance is the principle used by radios to tune to a specific station. Tuning to a frequency allows to receive only the information sent with that frequency, all other information is not accessible.

The same happens with life. We only perceive what vibrates at our own frequency. This resonance process allows information to flow. Every person, every event and every situation is associated with a specific vibration.

We communicate easily with people who have the same vibration as ours, while communication is more difficult with others. Individuals who resonate in the same way can easily establish lasting bonds. For example, young people who have had problems with abandonment, violence and abuse in their families tend to attract each other without knowing each other's history.

Resonance leads people to recognize themselves and to share feelings and information. This empathic communication process often takes place at an unconscious level.

We constantly experience resonance. We can talk to people of the same subject, using the same words, the same gestures and the same emphasis, and with some we feel that communication is full, while with others we feel that communication is empty.

Resonance allows to communicate at a deeper level. When we resonate we feel that communication is intense and positive.

The fundamental equations describe the present as the meeting point of causes that act from the past (causality) and attractors that act from the future (retrocausality).

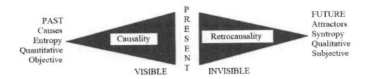

Causes are quantitative and objective and their effects are regulated by the law of entropy. Instead attractors are qualitative and subjective, their effects are governed by the law of syntropy.

The dynamic balance between entropy and syntropy presumes that any system vibrates between peaks of expansion and contraction:

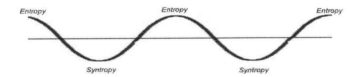

These cycles can be observed in any system and at any level, from the quantum level to the macro level and at the cosmological level where it supports Einstein's model of an infinite series of Big Bang and Big Crunch cycles.

In living systems resonance occurs with a significant involvement of emotions, this is called empathy. Empathy is an individual's ability to immediately understand the thoughts and feelings of another person.

When we study organizations we are always faced with two levels: the formal one which is the product of rationality and the informal one which is the result of resonance and empathy.

Formal and informal organizations coexist. It is impossible to eliminate the informal level, since it is based on natural processes of cohesion and resonance. The informal level can often be stronger than the formal level and must therefore be taken into due consideration in the management of any organization.

Organizations become cohesive thanks to resonance and informal networks. This can create great challenges for the management of the great pyramids which should accompany humanity during the ice age.

Formal organizations are a set of rules that establish the relationships between people, tasks and roles and determine the distribution of powers. These rules are codified in laws and agreements.

Instead, informal networks are fluid and spontaneous, based on resonance which allows people to identify each other. It attracts some elements and rejects others and leads to the creation of networks of which we can be part, knowingly or not, or from which we can be excluded. These informal networks follow the laws of life and nature.

When a person becomes part of an informal network, he can begin to resonate in a way that can lead to a reconfiguration of the network itself. Informal networks are redefined when new people are included or when people are excluded or leave. When people leave the resonance changes and the boundaries of the network are redefined. Sometimes it is simply enough for a person to leave to cause a real break of the informal network. Informal networks are strongly influenced by the people who are part of them, by their way of resonating, by their goals and visions. On the contrary, formal organization remains unchanged over time.

A continuous interaction between informal and formal is observed. Informal networks continually reinterpret and adapt procedures and rules. This reinterpretation facilitates the creativity, productivity and participation of people. When, on the contrary a strong pressure is exerted on the formal level, for example with the introduction of laws and controls that reduce the space for informal networks, there is a vertical drop in creativity, satisfaction and wellbeing. People give way to *"white strikes"* in which formal rules are meticulously respected, but in a way that reduces flexibility and creativity and the ability to respond to new problems.

- Duality and unity

Duality is everywhere: sexes, seasons, day and night, life and death, fullness and emptiness, movement and rest, pushing and pulling ...

The principle of complementarity states that every aspect of reality involves and contains its opposite. For example, whatever the degree of darkness of the night, there is always a part of the day. The night can be defined as the reduction of the day. Each polarity implies its opposite, as entropy implies syntropy and night implies day.

Polarities are like the labels "entry" and "exit" on the sides of a door. The unity is the door, the polarities are the sides from which we look at the door. The processes of perception lead to divide the unities into dualities. The dualities are therefore considered sequentially, thus transforming the unity into a flow of vibrations that can be perceived and managed by rationality and language. The flow of time becomes functional to the perception of these dualities. But the essence of reality remains unitary, even if we perceive it through the vibration of duality and believe that all aspects of reality are dual.

In other words, we do not see the door, but we see the two opposite signs "entry" and "exit" and we believe that this is reality. Depending on the angle from which we observe we see an aspect, but not the unity of polarities and their complementarity.

The transition from a dual to a unitary perception requires the harmonization of polarities. As long as we remain focused on one polarity we will continue to attract the opposite in our lives, because polarities are inseparable from each other, they are part of a unity.

For example, it often happens that a woman moves away from the influence of the authoritarian father by marrying an equally authoritarian man, or that a teenager may complain about his parents because excessively controlling and in turn becomes an authoritarian parent.

The principle of complementarity brings into our lives the very polarity we seek to exclude. For this reason it is said that the victim attracts his own executioner, an abused child evolves into an abuser and a masochist into a sadist.

When our vibrations remain the same we continue to attract what resonates in a similar way to us, even if in the opposite polarity.

Opposing polarities attract: women attract men, honest people attract dishonest people and so on. Good people do not realize that they vibrate in the same way as bad ones.

Due to the fact that the polarities attract each other, when we fight a polarity we are strengthening it and when we harmonize it healing begins.

Our tendency to take sides in the game of polarities stems from the identity conflict. The Theorem of Love offers the solution and shows that Love allows to move from duality to unity. This is why Love is so important in the healing process.

Whenever we get stuck in a polarity, in an attempt to provide meaning to our life, we are increasing the identity conflict, entropy and suffering.

Taking positions in this game of polarities increases suffering. Suffering signals that we must change course. We must not escape suffering or suppress it, but we must understand its message.

Anxiety and depression are warning signals, similar to those found in the cockpit of an airplane. In a cockpit, there is a large number of lights that turn on only when there is a problem that needs to be solved. If a warning signal is triggered, in the worst cases we must land at the nearest airport and ask for technical assistance. Obviously, this is annoying, but it makes no sense to blame the light that activated the warning signal, whose sole purpose was to inform us of something that required our attention.

The light that turned on forces to change plan, to land, to call for assistance, so that the journey can be resumed. If the technician removed the bulb of the light, instead of solving the problem, we would resume the flight with the light off, which is what we wanted, but the invisible problem would soon become visible as a serious technical problem.

Symptoms have the same function. If we deactivate symptoms using a drug, the "invisible" problem continues to act and over time develops into a more serious problem.

Symptoms often provide information on the polarity that we have tried to exclude, a valuable messages that shows how to solve the problem and what polarity we need to harmonize. Symptoms tell what is missing in our lives and what we need to acquire to restore the balance and integrity.

Symptoms and diseases reveal the polarity that we have excluded and have the function to help us evolve towards unity.

Since the time of Hippocrates, medicine has tried to explain symptoms by seeking causes in the past and attributing diseases to defects or functional causes. In doing so it lost sight of the message that is hidden in them.

Diseases are perceived as accidents and drugs are used to remove discomfort and suffering.

The goal is not to get rid of suffering, but to understand its message, the polarity that is missing in our lives and how we can restore our integrity.

When unity is restored, suffering vanishes. Suffering is not a fatality or a punishment, but a teacher ready to guide and help us.

As a good teacher who can show severity and hardness, when the message is finally received and transforms our life, symptoms disappears and gives rise to well-being.

True healing involves unity and a Love that binds all aspects of reality.

The polarities are inseparable. This is why it is sometimes necessary to choose the path of suffering to promote well-being. Suffering makes well-being visible, in a similar way to darkness that makes light perceptible. Suffering makes us recognize the path to wellness and has the power to show the way.

The much cited struggle between the forces of good and evil is not a struggle, but it is part of the evolution towards higher levels of awareness and truth.

Darkness cannot conquer light because light continually transforms darkness into light.

As Mephistopheles said:

"I am part of that force that always wants evil and always produces good."

We must learn to recognize the function of suffering and transmute it into Love and Truth, an invisible force that transcends the physical and leads to the unity of life and polarities.

EPILOGUE

We live in a world where everyone is in a "rat race" for pieces of paper with an imaginary value printed on. People work jobs they dislike to obtain these pieces of paper, attracted by consumerism, false needs and false narratives.

In 1284, while the town of Hamelin (Germany) was suffering from a rat infestation, a piper dressed in multicolored clothing promised that he could solve the problem. The mayor assured that for the removal of the rats he would pay the sum of 1,000 guilders. The piper accepted and with his music attracted the rats into the Weser River, where they all drowned.

Despite the piper's success, the mayor did not keep his promise and reduced the sum to 50 guilders, blaming the piper for bringing the rats himself in an extortion attempt.

Enraged, the piper swore revenge and on Saint John and Paul's day, while the adults were in church, he returned dressed in green like a hunter and playing his pipe. The 130 town's children followed him out of town and into a cave and were never seen again.

Only three children survived: one was lame and could not follow, the second was deaf and could not hear the music, the last was blind and was unable to see where he was going.

People are now being attracted, like rats, towards mass extermination in an attempt to keep them away from the scenario #2 of the ice age.

The third scenario where humanity as a whole survives, requires that we become deaf, blind and lame towards the music of these pipers.

Made in the USA
Middletown, DE
22 September 2019